HOW TO PADDLE A KAYAK

The 90 Minute Guide to Master Kayaking and Learn to Paddle Like a Pro

By Scott Parsons

*"The big question is whether you are going to be able to say a hearty **yes** to your adventure."*

- Joseph Campbell

Distinguished American writer and teacher

TABLE OF CONTENTS

INTRODUCTION

Rapids! Waterfalls! Churning water flowing downhill or along a shoreline! Glass-like stillness and a profound sense of peace!

Water has its own special allure and has drawn man for millennia. Many people now enjoy all types of motorized water sports, but a movement back to the tremendous sense of accomplishment of man against the elements through the experience of paddling is growing.

Find out how it all began as the history of paddling is described. Think about the transition of necessity into sport. There is not necessarily a lot to learn about paddling in order to go out and have fun, but there is always the option of *developing more advanced skills* with specialized equipment – even to the point of extreme white water! There is no intent to downplay safety and basic skills, but beginning to kayak can be done safely with some simple instructions and common sense.

The flow of this book allows you to truly start at the beginning if you have never experienced the pleasure of kayaking. It provides basic information about the *nature of kayaks* and how they function on the water. A basic overview provides some **guidelines for choosing the kayak** that will best suit your needs and **how to outfit** it to make your experiences safe and fun. Rudimentary *instructions for paddling* as well as *fitness suggestions* present a look at the physical requirements of the sport.

Once you have a better idea of the bigger picture, you will read about specific **paddling techniques** for both *river* and *sea kayaking*. Learn about the *hydrology* of a wild river and how to maneuver through obstacles as well as the skill of *reading the tides* and *winds* for kayaking through the surf. Finally, a brief look at the true excitement of kayaking demonstrates the extremes of the sport as a competitive event. Find out how others have **pushed the limits of kayaking** with specialized equipment and an almost fearless approach to the power of the water.

Websites, resources, and other links are included throughout the book for additional information and visual instruction of the topics covered in the text. Experts demonstrate skills step by step and offer advice and suggestions to make your beginning experiences easier. Please note, however, that no book or video is a true replacement for instruction from an experienced kayaker. That's not too difficult, though, since kayaking in a group is a terrific social activity and provides plenty of support and learning experiences.

Get out there and try kayaking to see if it is something you can enjoy! It may open up a new world of adventures for you!

CHAPTER 1 – KAYAKING FOR PLEASURE AND SPORT

Introduction to Kayaking

Paddling is more than simply climbing into a boat and paddling across the water. It is a wonderful *form of exercise*, provides the psychological benefits of relaxation and *stress reduction* along with the building of *self-esteem* through the achievement of learning a new skill. It is also an opportunity for *social interaction* with family and friends or the opening you need to join a club or group.

Mankind has been paddling for thousands of years. The earliest boats were simply logs that were hollowed out by fire or simple tools and did not have much maneuverability. They were also extremely difficult to transport over land. The Inuit peoples of the Arctic created what could be considered the first kayaks with separate materials; a framework covered with sealskin. Another example of early paddling craft are the Polynesian outriggers which were capable of covering great distances over the ocean.

Comparison Between Kayaks and Canoes

Kayaks and canoes are different based on the former's lower, narrower design, plus the top of the kayak is essentially closed. A canoe has a paddle with one blade, while a kayak is driven by a dual-ended paddle featuring two blades. The first 'modern' kayak was built by Englishman Rob Roy in the nineteenth century to paddle the inland waterways of Europe. Both types of boats have evolved during the past 200 years in terms of style and materials used. From the original hollowed-out trees, modern canoes and kayaks have become a precision craft designed for specific uses.

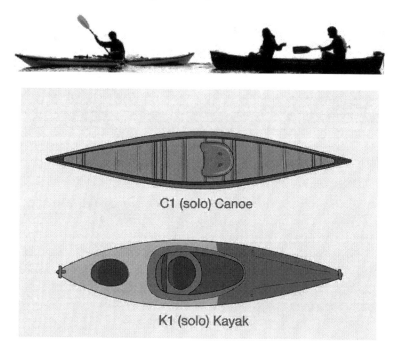

C1 (solo) Canoe

K1 (solo) Kayak

Basic Features of a Kayak

The evolution of the kayak into different lengths and widths began in the early twentieth century. The early Inuit kayak established the design of the current, long coastal kayak, but the needs of white-water and recreational enthusiasts modified that early craft. The various edge designs and hull shapes are filling multiple purposes including stability, speed, and maneuverability.

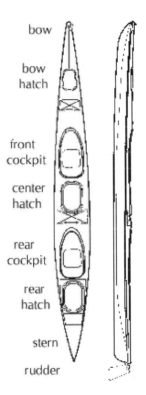

bow
bow hatch
front cockpit
center hatch
rear cockpit
rear hatch
stern
rudder

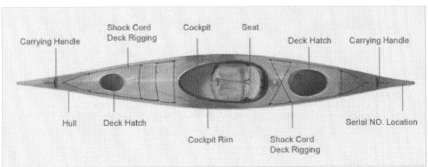

Carrying Handle
Shock Cord Deck Rigging
Cockpit
Seat
Deck Hatch
Carrying Handle
Hull
Deck Hatch
Cockpit Rim
Shock Cord Deck Rigging
Serial NO. Location

Different Types of Kayaks and Kayaking Experiences

There are a variety of kayaks available to enable a paddler to enjoy whichever type of kayaking that interests him. Touring kayaks and white-water kayaks have different characteristics that make them the most appropriate for your choice of venue. There are also differences within each type of kayak for specific benefits depending on the type of use the kayak provides. More details about the *different types of kayaks* will be found in <u>*Chapter 2*</u>.

Even though kayaking was originally the means to catch fish and seals in frigid northern waters, it has become an increasingly popular recreational activity. **Touring and white-water kayaking** are the two basic types of experiences available. **Touring** takes place on flat rivers, across lakes, in peaceful marshes, or along the shores of bays and the ocean. Nature is spread out around you from the beauty of a sunrise or sunset to the abundance of birds and wildlife and the expanse of woods or coastal plains.

White-water kayaking is just as rewarding in terms of beauty, but adds tremendous excitement as the kayak rushes over rapids challenging the paddler to pick his way through the river's obstacles and splashing water. Battling the water and coming down into a calm stretch is a thrill that makes you really feel alive.

Whether you crave the peace and serenity of a quiet lake or the exhilaration of a cascading stream, both types of kayaking are equally rewarding.

CHAPTER 2 - THE RIGHT STUFF: KAYAKING ESSENTIALS

Types of Kayaks

Equipment for almost any activity is available in a range of styles as well as sizes. The same is true for kayaks. **Touring kayaks** more closely resemble the Inuit boat that has been used for thousands of years. It is long – 4 to 5.5 meters – and tends to have a fairly flat hull with a streamlined, narrow bow and stern. This provides speed and ease in maintaining a straight course. **White-water kayaks** are quite different. They are much shorter – 1.8 to 3.4 meters – and have blunt ends and a broad hull for easy maneuverability in rough water.

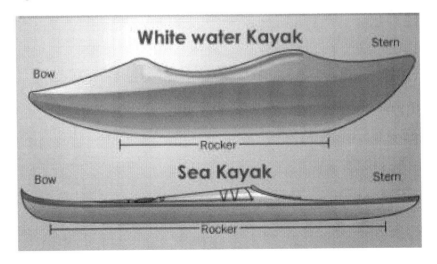

Within each category of kayak are multiple options that are designed for specific activities:

Touring Kayaks

- *Day Touring Kayak*: This is a basic style suitable for most recreational use on flat water and very minimal rapids.

- *Sea Kayak*: This is a longer style to more easily handle ocean swells.

- *Sit-on-top Kayak*: There is no open deck, but there is a seat and room for your legs molded into the deck covering. This is comfortable in warm water and weather.

- *Expedition Kayak*: This is a larger kayak intended for multi-day trips. The additional space can accommodate camping gear, clothes, and rations. These can also be fitted with additional gear such as GPS and lights.

- *Tandem Kayak*: As the name implies, two people can paddle together.

- *Foldboat*: This boat is made to fold for compact storage and transportation.

White Water Kayaks

- *Beginner's Kayak*: This is a kayak that provides the greatest stability with a combination of the features of white-water and touring kayaks. It is easier to maneuver than a touring kayak, but not as much so as a true white-water boat.

- *Slalom Kayak*: This is the type of kayak that is used in white-water competition; paddling a course similar to a downhill skiing slalom course.

- *Squirt Boat*: Designed in the 1980s as a white-water play boat, a squirt boat is not much more than a surfboard with a forward deck for a seat and leg room. This is a much more difficult kayak to handle for a beginner, so it should be avoided until the paddler gains basic white-water experience.

- *Inflatable Kayak*: These boats are exceptionally lightweight and ideal for difficult transportation and/or storage situations.

Kayaks that are referred to as '*recreational kayaks*' are a middle sized, relatively stable boat that can be used by beginners on easy white water or for short touring experiences. There is no special padding or molding for better seating that may be included in special purpose boats because recreational kayaks are used for general purposes and possibly by different people.

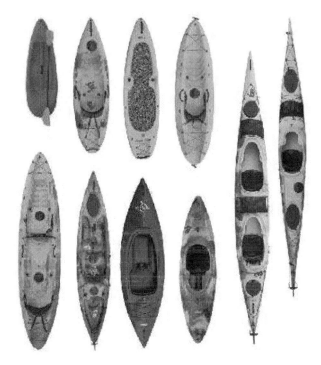

As you can see in this picture, the two longer boats on the right-hand side are best suited for the ocean and flat water because of their length and narrow lines. These are *touring* and *sea kayaks*. They are not suitable for white water, especially advanced conditions. All the kayaks can be used for flat water, and all the shorter boats (except for the first one, which is a *sit-on-top kayak*) are also suitable for easy white water and some more difficult conditions. These shorter kayaks are wider and have more rounded bows and sterns compared to the sea kayaks. Most of them can be classified as *recreational kayaks*.

Types of Paddles

Paddles come in almost as many sizes and shapes as the kayaks themselves do. You need to consider the **weight, durability**, and **material** used in the construction of the paddle as well as the **design** and **shape of the blade**. The most important factor, though, in choosing a paddle is the feel of it in your hands.

There is nothing that provides more of an outdoor feeling than using a *wooden paddle*. The downside to wood is the possible maintenance over time.

Other materials such as *fiberglass* and *carbon fiber* are also used for their strength and low weight, but a fiberglass shaft has an odd feel, and carbon fiber shafts – although, strong in certain respects – are fragile.

Cheaper paddles are available that are suitable for beginners. They include *plastic* and *aluminum* shafts with a synthetic blade. One great advantage to the aluminum paddles is that they are available in two parts so they can be easily stored and just as easily snapped together for use.

Using the **correct size paddle** is more important than the paddle's composition, with longer paddles used for touring and shorter ones used for white water. Divided into four basic categories, people who are under 5'2" (157 cm) should use a paddle that is 188-194 cm for white water and 210 cm for touring. The tallest group, 5'10" to 6'6", should use paddles of 200 cm and 230 cm.

Some manufacturers have created paddle shafts with different diameters so smaller hands can have a more comfortable grip. **Paddle shapes** can be chosen for speed and paddle sizes, such as large for surf, white water, and fitness, and smaller blades are available for smaller kayakers and people who want less stress on wrist joints.

Other factors to consider when choosing the best paddle for your kayaking plans include the **feathering of the blade** and the **angle of the shaft**, but these are matters of personal preference for experienced kayakers. Once you determine how advanced you want to become, you can make changes to your equipment.

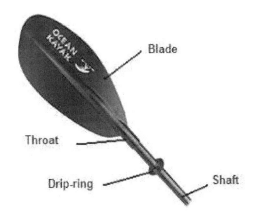

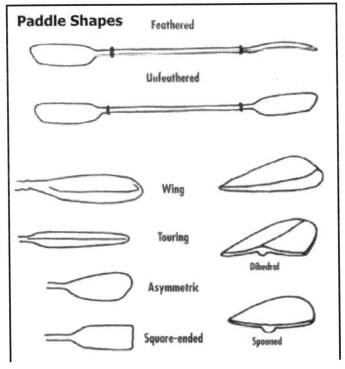

Personal Flotation Devices

This is the single, **most important piece of equipment** every paddler must have. It can't be stated strongly or often enough that any time you are paddling, you must wear a **PFD**. It's like a car safety belt – you don't want to be in the position of saying 'I wish I had worn it' or dead because you didn't.

There are five categories of life jackets and flotation devices approved for specific uses by the US Coast Guard. *Type III* floatation aids and *Type V* special-use devices are the most commonly worn by paddlers. The important factors to consider when choosing a PFD are the *fit*, *visibility*, and *buoyancy*.

- A PFD must **fit** snugly without impairing a free range of motion. It should not ride up when you sit or are in the water. Your chin should not rub against the top of the vest.

- Since a person in a kayak is very low in the water, **visibility** is a must. Bright colors are best so that other boaters or rescue personnel can easily see a paddler.

- **Buoyancy,** or the ability to keep you afloat, is determined by weight. Although usually associated with the size of the device, it is always a good idea to check the weight range listed for a particular device and make sure it is rated to hold your weight.

Correct Clothing Choices

Kayaking does not call for special clothing, but there are some **general principles** that should be kept in mind when **dressing for your kayaking experience**. For a short paddle around a pond or limited excursion along a lake shore or beach, a bathing suit should be enough, perhaps with a t-shirt over top. For extended paddling, however, it is good to follow the '3 Ws' – *wicking, warmth*, and *weather*.

Synthetic materials are the best because of their ability to dry quickly, provide warmth, and remain comfortable in the sitting position and while rotating your upper body as you paddle. There are numerous options for this first layer of clothing that include long and short sleeves and fabrics with UV and bug protection built in. Their purpose is to 'wick,' or remove, moisture from the body. Undergarments are also available with wicking capability.

Warmth is something you need to consider, even if it is a warm day. If not needed at first, clothing for warmth should be put into an airtight bag and stowed where it is accessible if it is needed. Since it is likely that you will get wet at some point on an excursion, having an extra set of dry clothes is a good idea. Extra layers of warmth as well as head-to-toe coverage need to be considered in cooler weather. Remember – the air may not feel cool, but the water can cause hypothermia quickly.

Even if the **weather** forecast calls for sunny skies, you never can tell, especially on the water. At the least, you will get splashed as you paddle, so a waterproof jacket is never a bad idea. You need to consider the wind and the likelihood of precipitation and be prepared. A cagoule is a special paddling jacket that comes in long and short sleeves that prevents water from getting under your clothes or through the deck skirt.

Footwear is also something to consider while kayaking. For the beginner, tennis shoes or sturdy sandals with straps should be enough. You will want to protect your feet from hidden dangers under water as well as rocks on the shore. Water shoes and neoprene booties are available that help keep out sand and stay on your feet better than other types of footwear.

Additional Accessories

Many other items can help make your kayaking trip more comfortable. You probably want to consider sun glasses to protect your eyes from the intense sun and the glare from the water. A hat or visor can help shield your face, and sunscreen should be applied to all exposed skin. Even cool or overcast days can set the stage for sunburn. A water bottle or two are always a good idea.

For specific situations, there are also specific pieces of equipment to consider. A **helmet** should always be worn for kayaking in white water. It is also a good idea if there is any chance of encountering rapids. It is easy to hit your head on an obstacle if you capsize, so a helmet can protect you from severe injury.

A **spray skirt** is handy for rough water where you are likely to take on water into the kayak. The spray skirt fits around the paddler's waist and stretches out and fits snugly over the rim of the kayak's cockpit. With the exception of sea kayaks, the interior stays dry and helps retain warmth. It is imperative to practice capsizing and performing a wet exit if you intend to use a spray skirt.

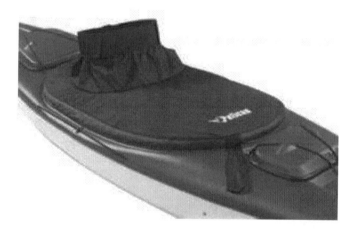

Some other basics that you should consider are a **first aid kit, dry storage,** an **extra paddle,** and **basic rescue gear.** (Note: rescue techniques and equipment will be explained more fully in later chapters. A list of first aid items appears in the appendices at the end of the book.)

Transporting the Kayak and Equipment

There is more to purchasing a kayak than adding paddles and other gear. You will also have to transport the kayak from the shop to your home and then to the launch site. The safest method for doing that is to buy *specialized roof racks*. Never drive with the kayak right side up because they are not aerodynamic in that position. **The best position is for the kayak to be on its side.** Especially, to hinder the rushing air and hold in the kayak's gear – such as paddles and safety equipment, cover the cockpit whenever you transport the kayak on your vehicle.

To move the kayak from the parking area to the water is not so difficult. Since they are extremely lightweight, many kayaks can be carried by one person with the cockpit rim on one shoulder. The toggle handles attached to the bow and stern of most kayaks enable two people to easily carry one or two kayaks together. *Fold-up trolleys* are also available to transport a heavily loaded kayak to the launch site. The trolley can then be dismantled and stowed in the kayak.

CHAPTER 3 - THERE'S MORE TO IT: CONSIDERING MOTHER NATURE

Where to Paddle

That seems to be a silly topic – the obvious response is 'on the water.' There are several different classifications for water in terms of safety and not all of them are safe for the novice. An advanced paddler can go virtually anywhere, but a beginner should restrict himself to the following three categories.

- **Quiet water** is just what the name implies. This is relatively calm, sheltered from wind, and not open to large motor boats. The paddler can quickly get the feel of the kayak in the water, the paddle in his hand, and the motion of the basic strokes. Entering and exiting the kayak is easier and practicing capsizing and rolling is more controlled.

- **Gently moving water** can be found in rivers, canals, or large streams with no obstacles or rapids and a negligible current. A paddler should be able to move upstream with little effort. A kayak only needs a depth of 6-12 inches (15-30 centimeters) to be able to maneuver, but a little more depth is better.

- **Lake inlets and outlets** are relatively shallow, marshy areas with generally calm water. These are wonderful places to be able to get close to wildlife without causing undue alarm, and many species of plants are easier to see up close. One disadvantage to marshy conditions is the thick mud bottom that makes capsizing particularly unpleasant.

For more advanced paddlers, or for novices under the guidance of an instructor, **larger lakes**, the **open seas**, and **white water** are venues for more exciting kayaking. The classifications of difficulty for coastal waters and rivers are listed in the appendices.

Reading the Water, Currents and Tides

Water has a special beauty whether it is smooth as glass or rushing and splashing over rocks. No matter what type of water you are attracted to, however, there is an element of danger. It is ***important to understand how 'to read the water.'*** As you look at a stream or river, you need to recognize what the signs of potential danger are by the way the water moves, swirls, and calms. In the sea or bays, the rising and falling of the tides and the way the currents move can be dangerous to someone not familiar with these movements.

In a river, the basic principle of gravity draws the water downstream. There are many factors that make it much more complicated than that, however. The width and depth of the river are two major considerations, but the bends of the river's course and the presence of obstacles also create changes in the main flow of the water. These will be discussed in the next section.

In the sea or even bays and estuaries that are affected by tides, there are a whole different set of factors to take into consideration. The current of a rising or falling tide may be stronger than that of a river and a surprise to a paddler who assumes all the water flows at the same rate. Some tides are gradual, but others are extremely steep, exposing many things at low tide that are not even suspected at high tide. The rip currents created on a beach pounded by the surf can help a paddler move offshore, but also prevent him from returning to shore.

No matter where you choose to paddle, it is important to find information about the water, dangers that may exist, and the locations of safe stopping sites. Books and charts are available, but an expert guide or instructor can provide the best advice.

Learning About Obstacles and Hazards

In natural conditions, the bed of a river is constantly changing. This creates differences in the flow of the water that can be used to a kayaker's advantage or hurt him if he is caught unaware. The most common situation is to find a *faster current in the center of the expanse of water with slower moving water closer to the banks.* When the river narrows, the water is forced through the opening faster. At a bend, the faster water is closer to the outside, so a paddler should aim the kayak to pass the inside of the curve and then take advantage of the faster flow as he comes around.

Rocks and boulders are the most common **obstacles in a river**, but the way the water moves around and over them has certain consistent features. Where the water flows between two rocks, a V-shaped chute is formed. The upstream V has higher water and can provide a cushion from the rock itself. The best course is the middle of the chute in the downstream V. The kayak will flow down the chute, and the paddler just needs to keep balanced and look ahead to the next chute. Submerged rocks can be identified by the rise in the water flowing over them. These 'pillows' are closer to the rock when the rock is closer to the surface. With practice, it becomes easy to read the difference and avoid the rocks that are just below the surface.

On the downstream side of particularly large rocks or a vertical drop, a phenomenon called a *hole* or *hydraulic* is formed. The water that has come over the obstacle goes to the bottom of the river. When the volume of water rising up and backwards to the obstacle is higher than the volume that continues downstream, the resulting current can hold back a kayak and force the paddler to work harder to continue downstream. If this hole is caused by a low-head dam, and the resulting backwash is more than a few feet, a paddler could be in serious trouble.

Eddies are larger areas of relatively still water in a downhill section of rapids. The obstacle is large enough to provide a protected section of water just downstream, but the edge separating the eddy from the downstream current can be rough and hazardous to a beginning kayaker. Learning how to enter eddies is an advantage so that you can take short rests in the course of a long stretch of rough water.

One of the most dangerous hazards encountered on a river is a downed tree or field of debris stuck between rocks. Because the water flows through the small openings, you may be caught against the strainer and drown. Strainers on the outside of river bends are particularly dangerous because that is where the faster current is drawn, making the obstacle harder to avoid.

In the event of capsizing, it is important to try and **position yourself upstream from the kayak**. This way, the kayak will not pin you to an obstacle.

Weather Awareness

Weather can be very fickle, especially over large bodies of water. Being prepared for the possibility of **rain** will not interrupt your trip or make you miserable. It is sometimes fun and particularly peaceful to paddle through the rain. If a strong **wind** blows up, it is best to get to shore because you will expend a tremendous amount of energy just to stay on course, and the water conditions may become rough enough to cause you to capsize. **Lightning** is a reason to get to shore immediately because it is attracted to an isolated object on the water faster than it is to one on land.

On the water, *hypothermia* is the deadliest situation a paddler can encounter. It is far too easy to get wet, and without proper planning, hypothermia will set in quickly if you cannot get dry or warm. So, it is vital that you are prepared for colder water and weather with extra layers of dry clothing for additional protection, which can be securely stowed in the kayak with you.

General Boating Etiquette

Just as there are rules for driving a car, there are also rules of the road for boaters. This is extremely important when you will be in an area where there are other boats or swimmers.

Because kayaks are small and generally easy to maneuver, it is up to the paddler to **give way to larger craft. The usual rule is to keep to the right and pass oncoming traffic to your left.** (This is like driving a car on the continent, not in England.) Should the kayaker find themselves in a narrow channel, close to other boats, it is appropriate for the kayaker to stay near the shore-side of buoys or navigational markers, then cross traffic as quickly as they can at a right angle and *only* when they are trying to reach a port or avoid an emergency. There are other rules of international navigation that involve sounding a whistle if sight is obstructed, if you are in fog, or if you are changing course relative to a larger vessel, but a beginning paddler should not be in any of those situations.

CHAPTER 4 – THE IMPORTANCE OF SAFETY PREPARATIONS

Know Your Skill Level

Kayaking for general recreation does not require any special fitness preparations, but it is always a good idea to have an idea of your basic physical capabilities. While most people think the arms or shoulders are the most important muscles for paddling, a strong core – abdominal and lower back muscles, among others – is responsible for correct paddling. This will be explained in greater detail in Chapter 5 and Chapter 7.

At this point, skill will be considered as not only a **basic fitness level**, but also as the degree of common-sense regarding **water safety** and **following directions**. Anyone who is afraid of the water or cannot swim is not a good candidate for learning how to kayak. Beyond that, someone who is not at all accustomed to physical exertion should probably begin with a general fitness program. Finally, if there is not a healthy respect for the power of running water or a casual approach to safety, kayaking is definitely not a good idea. The following skill level classifications can help you determine your capability:

- **First timer** – a paddler who has just begun and has a low level of experience and, maybe, confidence.

- **Beginner** – a paddler who has some experience can manage a kayak with basic strokes and handle Class I rapids.

- **Intermediate** – a paddler who can use a few advanced strokes along with all the basics can maintain control of the kayak in moderate waves and wind, handle Class II or III rapids, and can perform assisted rescues.

- **Advanced** – a paddler who has a good command of all paddling techniques, is confident in most water and weather conditions, can manage Class IV and V rapids, and perform self- and assisted rescues.

The person who assumes leadership of a group is responsible for the safety of everyone in the group. Never lie to yourself or to a group leader about your level of ability! You could put others at risk and probably not enjoy the experience yourself.

Know How to Avoid Capsizing

While there are many reasons for a kayak to capsize and dump the paddler into the water, there are some basic precautions to try and prevent that from happening. A kayak is, by nature, not a very stable craft. It is important to **keep your weight centered** in the boat and **avoid leaning over too far**. If something falls in the water, you can maneuver the kayak towards it and reach with the paddle to keep the bulk of your weight centered. When entering or getting out of a kayak, **three points of contact help maintain stability**. For example, two hands on the kayak as one foot steps in. Carrying gear is a necessity even on just a day trip but **never overload your kayak**. Gear should be stowed as close to midway in the boat, both side to side and front to back, and secured to avoid tumbling around freely.

What to Do if You Capsize

The first thing that needs to be stated is that **a PFD should always be worn when in a boat**. Even strong swimmers can be pulled under water and drown without a life-saving device. That false assurance of being a careful person or the water being calm does not rule out the possibility of capsizing, so knowing what to do is vital. A sudden dip in cold water can be disorienting, so practicing how to capsize and recover is an important part of learning how to kayak.

Capsizing near shore in calm water makes the paddler feel silly more than in danger. You should signal others that you have gone in the water and that you are all right. It is necessary to gather any gear that has begun to float away, especially the paddle. If possible, right the kayak and tow it to shore with the end line either by walking or swimming with a modified side stroke.

In moving water, you should try to make sure your body is on the up-river side of the kayak so you do not become trapped or crushed against an obstruction if you are in fact able to hang on. If the kayak is pulled away, the safest position is on your back with your feet pointing downstream. This protects your head from making first contact. If the water is not running too rapidly, try to backstroke to shore at a very gentle angle to keep your head upstream. It may be necessary to sidestroke aggressively towards shore, but watching for obstructions and protecting your head is crucial. This demonstrates the logic of wearing a helmet when kayaking in white water!

What NOT to Do
When You Capsize

The most important advice for someone who has capsized is ***do not panic***.

In calm water, do not let your equipment float away.

In moving water, ***do not stand up*** unless the water is less than knee deep. If you are knocked over, your head may end up downstream or a foot could become wedged under a rock.

Do not stay in the water longer than necessary, especially if it is cool or the weather is bad.

Also, do not attempt to re-enter the kayak if it is damaged or not stable. You could fall right back in!

Basic Rescue Techniques

If you are in open, relatively calm water and unable to tow the kayak to shore, it is relatively easy to accomplish alone if there is a paddle float. This is an inflatable sleeve that fits over the blade of the paddle to keep that end afloat while the other end is secured in the rigging across the kayak just aft of the cockpit. You should have one leg in the cockpit to make it easier to inflate the paddle float. With the paddle set as an outrigger on the up-righted kayak, pull your body up onto the stern deck, pivot so that you can put your legs into the cockpit one at a time, while turning and holding the paddle float for support. Re-establish correct posture and pump the water out of the kayak. Staying low over the boat keeps the center of gravity low so it is less likely to tip again.

If another kayaker is nearby, there are several options for performing a rescue. Instead of re-entering the kayak, the downed paddler can either hold on to the tow line or handle at the stern of the kayak, while the other kayaker tows the partially submerged boat to shore. If the swimmer is too tired or in a panic, he or she can 'hug' the rescue boat (wrap arms and legs around either end of the hull) and the unattended kayak can be towed or bulldozed to shore.

For an assisted rescue where the swimmer wants to re-enter the kayak, the two kayaks should 'raft up,' which means positioning them bow to stern and spanning both with a paddle. The seated kayaker can also hold the edge of the other cockpit to provide additional stability and the swimmer should re-enter the kayak the same way he would in an unassisted rescue. Re-establish correct posture, make sure the paddle is at hand, and pump out the water.

A kayak-over-kayak rescue involves the rescuer pulling the overturned boat over his deck to drain it. He then turns it over and returns it to the water parallel to his own boat, holding the cockpit for stability. The swimmer pulls himself onto his kayak like in 'rafting up.'

A rescue can be performed from shore with a brightly colored, floating tow rope thrown out to the swimmer in a throw bag. The rescuer should be sure of having secure footing before throwing the bag and even consider tying the free end of the rope to a stable object if the water is fast moving. The swimmer will be forced to the shore by the current and should be warned not to stand up until the water is lower than knee deep.

Universal Communication

Five basic messages are recognized universally by paddlers to share information over the sounds of rushing water. These are similar in concept to those used by soldiers on a silent patrol.

- **Stop** – Hold the paddle with both hands straight up over your head. Other paddlers should stop safely as soon as they can and wait for additional signals.

- **Help/Emergency** – The paddler can blow three long blasts on a whistle (which should be standard equipment attached to the life vest). With the paddle held up vertically, hand just above the lower blade, the paddler should wave the paddle side to side. Unless another paddler is specifically trained in emergency response, all paddlers should remain at a safe distance.

- **All Clear** – The paddle is held still with one hand, straight up in the air.

- **Directions** – Hold the paddle vertically, straight and high, in the direction to proceed. This should always be to the clear path, *not* towards an obstacle or hazard.

- **Are You OK?** – With the hands, point to the person in question and tap the top of your head three times.

Planning a Trip

The first step in planning a group trip is to know the ability levels of the participants and the level of difficulty of the proposed route. It is always best to have experience on the water you plan to paddle with a group. Awareness of the weather is also important because unanticipated rain, wind, extreme cold or heat can change a pleasant trip into a miserable one.

Along with personal experience, talking with others who have experience in that area is beneficial as are guidebooks and local maps. Before heading out, the concept of working as a group needs to be clarified. This includes co-responsibility for maintaining communication, watching for obstacles, and practicing personal safety and responsibility. Roles for other specific functions are then assigned. These roles include:

- **Trip leader** – assumes overall responsibility for the group, preparations, and knowledge of the proposed route. The leader essentially calls the shots – carries the map, compass, safety and rescue gear, repair kit, and extra paddle. This person should have knowledge of the medical or physical limitations of any group member and assign a second-in-command to provide backup or help.

- **Sweep** – should have strong skills and the ability to perform rescues. This paddler brings up the rear to keep an eye on the whole group.

- **Rescue** – all paddlers should understand that the two kayaks closest to someone in trouble are the initial responders. Other paddlers not involved in the rescue should pull over and wait or help if necessary.

Everyone is responsible for carrying their own necessary gear and any extra can be divided up among group members. (See Chapter 2 about equipment.)

All the same guidelines apply for an extended trip and a short trip. For a longer excursion, the addition of camping gear and extra food is the major consideration. Group members should take on particular tasks in preparation for the trip, and all the rules for specific functions within the group accepted. There is a higher level of endurance required for long trips, so physical condition and limitations need to be seriously assessed and accounted for. There should be designated contact persons in the event of needing to get information 'home,' and a 'float plan' should also be left with someone on land to keep track of the progress of the trip.

CHAPTER 5 - BEFORE YOU GET IN THE WATER

Personal Fitness

A kayaking trip you can enjoy requires a certain level of physical fitness. Having good physical fitness can make the difference between being able to save yourself and others or waiting on someone else to help, and putting off paddler fatigue, which often ends up in poor decision-making along with unintentionally losing control of the kayak. Solid physical fitness is needed to help avoid injuries.

There are four elements that support a necessary measure of fitness for kayaking. A certain amount of **strength** is needed to carry the kayak to the water or portage around unnavigable obstacles. Strength is also needed to complete rigorous paddle strokes, especially in white-water situations.

Additionally, **flexibility** is a factor in performing the most effective paddle strokes and lessens the likelihood of stiffness. A strong core is an important element of the flexibility required for paddling. While strength and flexibility enable the paddler to perform effective strokes, **endurance** is required for longer or more strenuous trips. Sustaining an effective level of endurance – the capability to exert yourself without immediate fatigue or heart strain – will delay, or even prevent, physical exhaustion that often puts a paddler and others at risk. **Cardio-respiratory fitness** has a direct effect on your physical stamina. Your body and your muscles function better when they receive well-oxygenated blood. In a worst-case scenario, too much exertion and stress could lead to a heart attack.

Warming Up

To prepare for a trip in your kayak, it is a good idea to spend a little time performing some simple stretches for each set of muscles, beginning at the head and working down to the toes. These exercises are also good for everyday routines and off-season training. To get more out of some elements of your stretching routine, use a paddle or some stationary object for support and resistance. The idea of these movements is to gently stretch your muscles, not to strain them. Use slow, steady pressure for each.

- **Head and neck** – Gently lean your ear to the shoulder, using your hand on the same side for additional pressure. Switch to the other side and repeat.

- **Shoulders** – Lift your arms, making a straight line with your shoulders, then rotate them in tight circles, moving forward for a while, then backward.

- **Triceps** – With one arm over your head, bend it at the elbow to reach behind your neck. With the other hand at your side, bend the elbow to reach up behind your back. Each hand should clasp the fingers of the other hand and gently pull. Switch arms and repeat. Another option is to raise one arm up and bend it at the elbow so your hand is touching the back of your neck or upper spine. Use the other arm to gently add pressure to the arm as if to get it to reach farther down your back. Switch and repeat.

- **Biceps and forearms** – Extend one arm out straight in front of you with the palm facing up. With the other hand, grasp the fingers and pull on them, keeping both arms straight.

- **Chest** – Put your hands behind your back, one hand holding on to the opposite wrist. Keeping the arms as straight as possible, lift your hands alternating hand to wrist positions. Another option is to brace your straight arm raised almost to shoulder height and push against the brace, while rotating your body away from it. Alternate arms.

- **Back** – Cross your straight arm over your chest and catch it with the other arm, which should be bent at the elbow with the fist up. Use the bent arm to press the straight arm back into the chest. Alternate sides.

- **Core** – This demands special attention because it is the source of power and the performance of the most effective paddling strokes. You will be stretching front to back and side to side. With your hands on your hips and feet shoulder width apart, slowly bend straight back from the waist, while maintaining a normal breathing pattern, then lean forward the same way. With your hands on top of your head and your feet shoulder width apart, slowly lean to the side from the waist without leaning forward, return to the upright position and repeat on the other side.

- **Quads** – Stand comfortably up straight. Keeping your knee pointing to the ground, raise one flexed foot up towards your butt and hold the position. Slowly lower your foot and repeat the procedure with the other foot. Use a support to maintain your balance.

- **Gluteal muscles** – While stretched out on your back, bend one knee and raise it to your chest using both hands to apply gentle pressure. Slowly straighten that leg and repeat with the other.

- **Groin** – With your legs spread farther apart than shoulder width and keeping your back straight over your center of gravity, place both hands on your upper thigh as you bend that leg so it is bearing your weight. Hold the position, slowly return to the upright position and lunge to the other side.

- **Hamstrings** – Without locking your knees, stand with your feet wider than shoulder width apart, bend forward from the waist, and try to grab your ankles (or the back of your legs, as far down as you can). Return to the upright position and repeat the process, but alternate between holding each ankle separately after each upright position.

- **Calves** – Either starting from a standing position and putting your hands on the ground or from a kneeling position with your hands on the ground in front of you, form an overturned V with straight arms and legs, applying pressure equally over your hands and feet.

- **Ankles** – While standing or sitting, extend a leg out so the foot is off the ground and slowly rotate the ankle to perform circles both clockwise and counterclockwise. Switch legs and repeat.

It is also a good idea to test your range of motion in the kayak while wearing a PFD. Perform some simple torso twists and side-to-side and back-and-forth stretches. After a day of paddling, cooling off with the warm-up stretches helps to prevent stiffness.

Off-Season Fitness

Unless you participate in kayaking excursions in extreme conditions or in exotic places all around the world, you will probably have an 'off season.' Don't let that downtime ruin any physical conditioning you have gained in the course of kayaking! There are plenty of opportunities to stay in shape so your body is ready for the next kayaking adventure.

Cross training is the best way to keep fit for paddling. There are *cardio activities* to support endurance and proper blood oxygenation and *strength exercises* to keep muscles in good shape. *Swimming* is an excellent exercise because it works on both aspects of fitness. It gets your blood flowing faster, works many muscle groups, and aids flexibility. Combining swimming with basic diagonal crunches, push-ups, and pull-ups that are easy to do anywhere help maintain fitness. Other activities such as aerobics or jogging, bicycling on the road or in the gym, and a variety of weight and resistance activities that mimic the motions of paddling will keep you interested in the routine and hopefully enable you to have some fun at the same time.

Nutrition and Hydration

For someone to maintain physical fitness and mental alertness, it is crucial to **eat a balanced diet** and **drink plenty of water**. If you are anticipating a particularly strenuous outing, more calories will be burned than if you are paddling along a calm river or still lake, so you may need additional food to supply the energy. Calories derived from fresh fruits, vegetables, and whole grains are the most beneficial to your body along with lean meats and fish or some other protein substitute. On a day trip or longer excursion, snacking on some fruit, 'trail mix,' as well as something salty keeps your blood chemistry in line so you remain alert and can focus without suffering from hunger. Similarly, adequate hydration is needed to avoid confusion and tiredness. Roughly 200-250 ml of water should be consumed every 20-30 minutes throughout the trip. It is almost impossible to drink too much water, but it is surprisingly easy to become dehydrated.

CHAPTER 6 - GETTING WET: YOUR FIRST STEPS IN KAYAKING

Getting into the Kayak

The most basic way to enter the kayak is by placing the bow in the water and keeping the stern on land. Then, sit on the kayak's back deck, aim your feet into the cockpit, and slowly slide your legs into the boat until you are seated. With a little shifting side to side and a push with the paddle, you are afloat.

If the beach is too rocky, the bank is elevated, or you don't want to risk damaging an expensive boat, the procedure will be slightly different. The kayak will be placed in the water parallel to the water's edge, and one end of the paddle will rest on the shore, while the other extends across the kayak behind the cockpit. With most of your weight against the paddle shaft and the cockpit's back rim, slowly shift from a crouching or sitting stance on land into the kayak, then extend your legs and assume the correct paddling position. When launching from a dock, you will also use this technique depending on the height of the dock relative to the kayak.

No matter what the circumstances are regarding the location of your entry into the kayak, there are several ***basic rules to always bear in mind***:

- Move cautiously and smoothly, not abruptly.
- Maintain three points of contact – two feet and one hand, two hands and one foot.
- Keep a low center of gravity as much as possible.
- Hold on to the paddle.

- Centralize yourself in the kayak.

The *seal launch* is another technique for a dry entry in which the more advanced paddler is already seated in the kayak, prepared to go. Using a low rock ledge or slanted bank over the water, the paddler pushes himself forward with his hands and lands in the water looking like a seal entering the ocean.

These techniques should be practiced in the calmest conditions possible and with the assistance of at least one other person so the actions become comfortable and smooth. They would also be covered during lessons by a certified instructor.

Landing and exiting the kayak involve these same basic techniques, which actually differ only slightly for sea launchings and landings.

Correct Seating Position

Good posture is essential to promote effective paddling and minimize back strain or even injury. This does not mean rigid military posture, but rather sitting with your back relatively straight, chin up, shoulders back comfortably, and arms resting loosely at your sides. This should make you think of your mother or piano teacher telling you not to slouch. A strong and flexible core makes this a natural position.

Many recreational kayaks are equipped with a back rest or even a back strap, but that is only meant for moderate support in the correct seating position – not a surface to lean all your weight back on. Lounging back is just as bad as slouching. For advanced kayaking, foam may be molded to adjust to your legs to help hold them in position.

Except for sit-on-top or racing kayaks, your legs will extend under the deck. There are adjustable foot rests that should be set so your feet rest against them and your knees are slightly bent and angled to the sides of the cockpit. In this position, there is less strain in your thighs and lower back, and your knees help to provide balance.

Balance

Balance was discussed briefly in Chapter 4 in the section "How to Avoid Capsizing," mostly in respect to loading the boat. The buoyancy and stability of each kayak is different depending on overall length, beam (width) above and below the water, and the shape of the hull. Some kayaks offer greater *initial stability*, or a greater range of lean and stability sitting still, or greater *secondary stability* that makes them less stable at entry but more stable underway. This section will discuss balancing skills the paddler must learn and practice for encountering the different types of water that might be present on a trip.

The key features for maintaining balance in a kayak are ***remaining loose, keeping your upper body centered in the kayak, and not overextending***. If you stiffen your body, you are working against the kayak instead of functioning as an integrated part of it. In calm water, it is good practice to experiment with different body movements in the kayak so you can develop a feel for the boat and the water. This is where the differences between initial and secondary stability can be identified.

Different ways in which your body leans will exert different forces on the kayak relative to the center of gravity. While it is usually best to keep your chin and spine in line with the center of the boat, various water conditions may require the paddler to lean a certain way to utilize current or the waves.

- **The body lean** is the easiest for a beginning paddler to use. It simply means leaving your butt basically flat on the seat, while you bend sideways from the waist. This does nothing to effect the stability of the boat but is difficult for some beginners to get past.

- **The bell buoy lean** is similar except that you shift your weight to one hip and maintain a straight spine – no bending at the waist. This position will result in capsizing if not corrected.

- **The J-lean** involves jutting your ribs to one side, while lifting the opposite knee and hip and keeping your head over the center of the boat. Your neck will be bent slightly toward the raised hip or away from the side of the lean. This maneuver allows a paddler to balance the kayak without the aid of the paddle so that he can concentrate on strokes for turning and power.

These moves are the elements on which advanced skills are based. Learning and practicing them at the beginning assures you of a quick transition to white water.

Basic Paddle Grip

For optimum performance, there are rules for holding the paddle just as there are rules for holding a golf club or bow and arrow. The correct grip makes the whole process more efficient. Learning that grip and using it every time you pick up the paddle will cause that paddle to become an extension of your arm through which you can feel differences in the water and the effect of your strokes.

To **_grip the paddle correctly_**, grasp the shaft with both hands over your head and your elbows at right angles (90 degrees) equal-distant to the blades. Your dominant, or control, hand should have a straight wrist and the power (concave) side of the blade should be facing the water. Bring the paddle and your arms straight down in front of you without loosening the control hand. The blade on the control side should now be vertical with the power side of the blade facing forward. Without using a death grip, the control hand should never allow the paddle to rotate – that is done solely by the opposite hand. Transferring this grip into a stroke will occur in the next chapter.

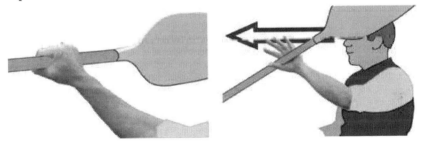

Practice Capsizing/ Righting the Kayak

Although it is very frustrating to think that you have been doing all this preparation and have still not moved anywhere in the kayak, it is vitally important to experience each of these steps to insure your safety on the water. Another important skill to practice before actually needing it is **how to capsize the kayak, get out of it**, and then **get back into it**. A qualified instructor or an experienced partner can help you do this so that it becomes an automatic response.

The first rule about capsizing may seem counter-intuitive – do not try to get out of the kayak as it is going over! Curl your body forward and stay in the boat until it is completely turned over! It is imperative that you stay calm so that you don't use up too much oxygen or lose it altogether. If it seems a little intimidating to roll in calm water, just imagine what would happen moving downstream!

As soon as the kayak is upside down, bang on the sides a few times as hard as you can to attract attention and wave your arms, signaling for help. After a few seconds, you are ready to exit the kayak.

The Wet Exit

The easiest and safest way to exit from a capsized kayak is to maintain a forward curl position with your chin tucked towards your chest. This not only makes the process faster, but helps to protect your head from underwater obstacles. Then, perform a forward roll motion holding on to the kayak with one hand and drawing your legs smoothly out of the cockpit.

If you are wearing a spray deck, wait until you are oriented upside down, hold the paddle to your midsection, pull the handle to release the cover, and draw your legs out. You should perfect this move first without using the spray deck, then practice with it.

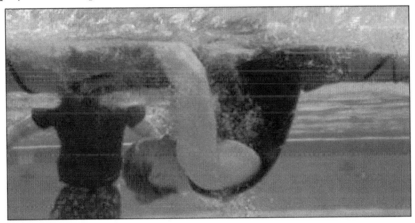

With the aid of the PFD, you will easily come to the surface. Hopefully, you still have hold of your paddle and the kayak and can either head for shore, have another kayaker assist you, or perform an unassisted rescue as discussed in Chapter 4.

Rolling

As a safety measure in the Arctic, Inuit Indians learned how to roll their water craft as a way of avoiding getting out into the cold water after capsizing. When it is done frequently enough, it becomes an almost continuous motion – hence the name 'Roll.' The process has developed into numerous different techniques, but they are all based on the same general principles.

From the 'start position,' where you are gripping the paddle in both hands alongside the kayak, lean to that side until you capsize.

Once you are completely turned over, elevate your back arm out of the water onto the back of the kayak.

Sweep the front paddle in a large arc across the top of the water and arch your back to the rear deck as you continue the sweep.

While bending from the waist to continue bringing the kayak around, keep your head back along the deck until the kayak is righted, then sit up.

The same roll can be done with a brace motion instead of a sweep. Bracing is discussed in Chapter 7.

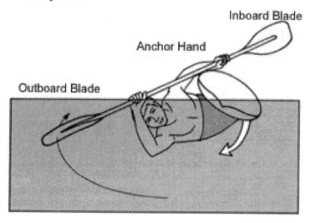

CHAPTER 7 – GETTING MOVING: DIFFERENT PADDLE STROKES

Forward and Backward Strokes

Before describing specific strokes, there are *several basic pointers to always keep in mind*:

- It's all in the torso! The rotation of your torso and shoulders supplies the power and reach for each stroke.

- Maintain control of the paddle! Keeping a secure grip with the control hand and allowing rotation in the opposite hand maintains the effectiveness of each stroke.

- Don't drown the paddle! A silly statement, but it serves to point out that the blade of the paddle should remain underwater during the power phase of the stroke, but as close to the surface as possible, except for particular exceptions.

For a good **forward stroke**, you need to insert the blade cleanly into the water as close to the edge of the kayak as possible with the power side of the blade at a right angle to the direction of motion. Your lower arm should remain straight until the very end of the stroke.

Pull on the lower shaft as it is staked into the ground and move the kayak forward.

Use your upper hand to push against the upper part of the shaft, keeping that elbow below or just at shoulder level. By the end of the stroke, that arm will have come across in front of your face.

With rotation of the torso, continue to bring the lower blade alongside the boat back to your hip. The upper hand will drop down, and the lower elbow will begin to bend.

At this point, you will be simultaneously lifting the lower arm and extending the opposite arm forward and straight to be ready for the next stroke.

The **backward stroke** is essentially the same thing in reverse. You *do not* change your grip on the shaft of the paddle. Turn your torso as much as you can so that you will be able put the paddle blade as far back as you can.

With the paddle close to the edge of the boat, draw it back through the water as you 'untwist' your torso.

When the blade reaches your feet, you will begin rotating to the opposite side to be ready to plant that blade in the water.

Remember to keep the water arm straight so you are truly transferring the power of your core to the paddle.

Stopping

Stopping a kayak goes beyond not moving the paddle. Achieving a complete stop requires the paddler to **drop the blade in the water** right next to the boat, making the paddle blade **perpendicular to the boat**. Keep the paddle straight until resistance turns the boat. Then, drop the paddle blade into the water on the opposite side. Repeat this process until the boat has stopped.

Forward and Reverse Sweep Strokes

The **forward sweep stroke** is the common way **to turn the kayak**. It can be used in the steady rhythm of paddling to alter course without missing a beat.

To make a more specific turn, reach forward with the blade as far as you can and stick it in the water. Rather than running the paddle along the kayak's side, reach with a straight lower arm to pull back the paddle with an arc.

The water blade will come back, near the stern, then flip the paddle and lift it out of the water. Do not let the blade hit the side of the boat!

If the blade comes up clean, and the boat remains stable, your kayak will keep turning.

Another technique that provides better motion with this stroke is to **'edge' the kayak**. This involves changing your balance slightly by lifting your knee on the up side of the paddle and shifting weight to the water blade side. This is similar to but much less exaggerated than a 'J-lean,' which was mentioned in Chapter 6.

The **reverse sweep stroke** works in the opposite way to the forward sweep stroke, but it will effectively slow forward motion.

Maintaining your grip on the paddle, as explained for the backward stroke, put the paddle blade in the water as far back as you can, then shift your shoulders and torso to achieve maximum extension.

Rotating effectively from your torso will help you pull the water blade forward through a wide arc. Remove it from the water before it can strike the kayak's bow.

When these sweep strokes are both used, the kayak will turn more quickly.

Draw Stroke

This stroke is intended for **moving the kayak sideways**. You start by rotating your body, aiming yourself in the direction you want to go.

Extend the paddle as far as you can from the kayak's edge, while making sure the power face of the blade is facing the boat.

Lift your knee on the paddle side and draw the paddle in towards the boat with the power arm as straight as possible and the paddle held in a vertical position.

As the paddle is nearing the side of the boat, use your wrists to change the angle of the blade 90 degrees in an underwater recovery.

Without taking the blade out of the water, push the paddle out away from the boat to the position you started in.

This stroke has to be done straight and at a central point along the kayak to avoid turning.

Stern and Bow Rudder

The **stern rudder** movement is used only for **slight adjustments to the direction of the kayak**. It is not intended to turn the boat – a forward sweep is the best way to do that – or stop it.

The paddle is placed as far back as you can comfortably reach with a straight lower arm. The drive face of the blade is facing the kayak and is held in place only long enough to effect the course correction.

A **bow rudder**, on the other hand, is a very commonly used stroke, especially in white-water conditions. It is, however, a more advanced stroke since it depends on several different movements and a good feel for the changes different blade angles create. It requires more strength, especially in the wrists and forearms.

Bracing

Low and high braces are **maneuvers used to** help a tipping kayaker **regain stability**. The paddle is used to provide just enough support to keep the kayak upright, while the paddler uses leg and hip movements to stabilize the kayak.

The **low brace** is done by laying the paddle on top of the water with the drive face up. The paddle is kept low with both hands lower than the elbows. More support is provided if the blade is farther away from the kayak. The paddler's weight is temporarily supported by this brace to provide time for him to stabilize the boat.

The **high brace** involves holding the paddle under the surface of the water with the drive face down. The hands should be above the elbows and not extended forward. This brace is more powerful than the low brace and, as such, puts a tremendous amount of strain on the shoulders. It should never be used in white water or even rapids because it is possible for the blade to strike something or get pulled down unexpectedly and that could lead to injury of the non-water shoulder.

These moves should be practiced and mastered because they are important elements used in rolling and all advanced paddling.

An excellent animated tutorial for beginning skills can be found at kayakpaddling.net

CHAPTER 8 – SEA KAYAKING

Launching and Landing

Getting into a **touring** or **sea kayak** is roughly the same as a recreational craft on calm water. The obvious difference is that you may have to consider working with waves on the sea. Most public launching areas are in protected inlets, but it is important to know how to deal with waves if you are touring along open coastline or small islands.

For any **entry into surf**, place the kayak close to the edge of the water where it is not affected by the wave action. The bow should be just touching water when the wave rolls in.

Make sure all gear is secured and quickly get into the boat. Fasten the spray deck and be sure to hold on to the paddle.

Push yourself with your hands into the water, keeping the kayak pointing directly into the wave line. If the boat gets pushed sideways back to shore, it will probably result in capsizing.

Landing a kayak through the waves uses the opposite approach to surfing. As a wave passes under you, begin to paddle behind it. Get on top of it at the very end for an extra boost onto the sand.

Try to push yourself further up the beach and get out quickly, holding on to the paddle. Keep a hold on the boat as well so the next wave doesn't carry it back out

Specialized Equipment

Long-distance paddling requires some variations on the general equipment needed for recreational or white-water kayaking.

- The *touring kayak* is longer and narrower.

- The long-distance *paddle* is also longer and may be lighter. A paddle shaft with a slight bend near the blades can help you avoid wrist strain.

- The *spray deck* may be nylon or a combination of a neoprene deck and nylon body sleeve.

- Offshore trips require *extra safety gear* such as a strobe emergency light, flares, and a VFH radio or mobile phone. A tow line and/or climbing slings should be standard equipment.

- *Clothing* should be worn in layers to account for the temperature changes in the course of the day. A dry suit may be needed in extremely cold situations, and outer waterproof gear is always a good idea.

Different Strokes

One tremendous difference in holding the paddle for long distances is called the **'slide hand.'** A shorter paddle can be used to create less wind resistance and a smaller profile, just for a strong wind to catch and pull out of your grasp.

The upper hand grasps the paddle at the throat of the upper blade. The 'water' hand holds the center of the paddle and guides the stroke like a normal forward or sweeping stroke.

At the end of the stroke, the paddle has to be slid to the other side and the water hand is now holding the throat of that end of the paddle.

Any touring paddle can be used in this manner except for one with a bent handle.

The **knifed-J stroke** is used when the conditions are windy and the boat gets pushed to the side at the end of every stroke when the paddle is lifted. To perform this stroke, turn your wrist at the end of the stroke so the blade faces the boat. This allows you to bring the paddle back to the front position easily as the turned blade knifes through the water. The blade also continues to hold the kayak in a straighter line since it is functioning as an element of the kayak through your good seating and grip.

The **figure eight stroke** is used for inside turns and begins the same way as the knifed-J stroke. When the paddle has cut through to the front position, the wrists are turned the opposite way to present the drive face of the blade to the bow and the back is used to complete the next stroke.

Note: this is another example of the benefits of getting to know the feel of the paddle and movement of the kayak in different situations.

Another drastic difference when paddling in a touring kayak is capsizing. Instead of righting the kayak to re-enter it, you perform an ***underwater entry***. This is due to two circumstances; a touring kayak is too unstable to do a standard upright re-entry, and less water is in the kayak when you turn upright. To keep your paddle handy, secure it under the deck lines spanning the kayak. This will help stabilize the kayak as you do the re-entry.

To achieve this re-entry, you have to get under the kayak, hold the cockpit with both hands and your head pointing to the bow. Hold yourself at arm's length and bring your knees to your chest so you can put your feet into the boat. Reattach the spray deck, get the paddle, and roll upright.

Understanding the Wind, Waves and Tides

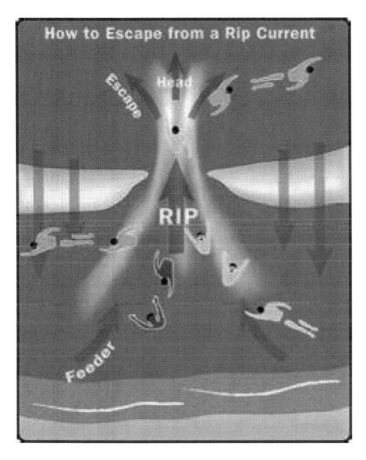

The tide and winds can be dangerous to a beginning kayaker. Ebb and rip tides prevent you from returning to the shore easily, and wind not only pushes you off course, but also raises the height of the waves. Other conditions create troughs that seem to trap you. Detailed charts and tables can provide you with basic information about the area so that the safest route may be planned, but not all water movements are accounted for on paper.

To learn how to handle these conditions, it is best to go with an instructor or other highly experienced paddler.

To put some of the information about the wind in perspective, the **Beaufort wind scale** rates the force of the wind into 12 categories. A beginning paddler should not go out in wind over level 2 or 3. Level 2 breezes are measured at 4-7 mph or 7-11 km/h. Level 3 is 8-12 mph and 12-19 km/h. Whitecaps can form at level 4 but most commonly at level 5. A level 6 wind blowing over the ocean for two days can create waves up to 18 feet or 5.5 meters high. Level 7 is considered near-gale force, and level 12 is the minimum wind speed for a storm to be classed as a hurricane.

Offshore waves are categorized two ways. **Chop** is created by brief winds blowing over a small area that create random waves. The best thing to do in this condition is to remain calm and loose and continue to paddle through. They make a bumpy ride but, because they pop up all around, don't exert much force on the kayak.

Swells, on the other hand, are the large rolling waves created by wind blowing over the ocean for great distances in the same direction. They are affected as they approach the shore by the direction and strength of the wind. If the wind is offshore (from land to the ocean), the waves become steeper and break in a crash. Lee, or following, winds press down on the tops of the waves so the water is just pushed off the forward face of the wave.

With other conditions affecting the characteristics of offshore sea water, such as tides or the mouths of bays and rivers, it is important to learn about these conditions before setting out on a trip.

Navigation and Buoys

Navigation includes having equipment to help you find your way and knowing how to use it. A *compass* and *map* should be adequate for most trips since people seem to follow the coast or shoreline. If you plan on crossing a more open stretch of water where the use of visible landmarks is limited, a compass, chart, and prior examination of the area are required. Seek out an expert, someone who knows the local area and who can share information about the waters you plan to paddle.

Navigation charts show land, the main channels in the waterways, and tide and navigational marker information. The color red is always associated with a pointed marker, and green is rectangular. The simple way to know which way to go through them is the phrase 'red, right, returning,' which is universally meant as keeping the red markers on your right side as you are returning to port. Other specialty markers are used in crowded waterways, intersections, or around sunken or natural obstacles.

The best way to understand navigation as well as basic seamanship is to take a class offered by maritime organizations.

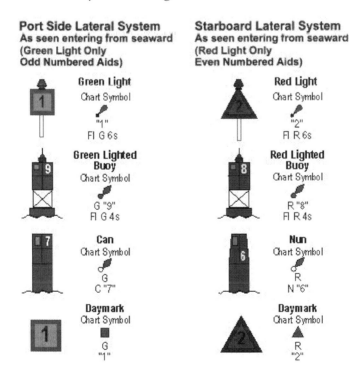

CHAPTER 9 – WHITE-WATER KAYAKING

Launching and Landing

Unless there is absolutely no calm water along the river you plan to paddle, a regular kayak entry should work. If there is no alternative than putting in along moving water or an eddy, it is best to have someone else there to help hold the kayak. You don't want to rush getting settled, putting the spray skirt on, or planning your initial path.

There are a few differences as you launch in moving water. The current may take you quickly due to helical flows of water that draw water from the shore toward the main current. An eddy may start you upstream, so you need to know how to maneuver in that situation. These techniques will be detailed later in this chapter.

The *seal launch* was mentioned in <u>Chapter 6</u>, but a quick review doesn't hurt. For the sake of safety, make sure the water is at least 3.5 feet or 1 meter deep for a forward seal entry. With the kayak on an overhanging bank, get yourself settled, the spray skirt attached, and your paddle ready. Push yourself forward into the water with one hand and the paddle in the other, and you are on your way.

An alternative to the seal launch is to place the kayak along the bank or a ledge and push off sideways to land flat in the water. This is the option to use if the water is not deep enough.

With more experience, you will get the feel for these launches and gradually be able to increase the height from which you push yourself into the water.

Specialized Equipment

A variety of different kayaks and paddles are available for white-water kayaking, depending on the type of moves you are planning to do. For a beginner, a general-purpose recreational kayak and paddle should be fine until certain techniques are mastered that enable him to do slalom, freestyle, or racing kayaking.

- *Protective gear and clothing* are the most specialized for white water. A good PFD is essential, but even at that, different styles are suited for specific purposes and a general purpose, recreational PFD is not adequate for advanced white-water kayaking. A helmet must be worn as well as a spray skirt.

- For *body warmth and protection*, a variety of products are available. *Wetsuit pants* are common for paddlers in cold water. A *cagoule*, which is a jacket designed specifically for paddling, fits over layers of several shirts of light- to mid-weight fabric and is perfect for keeping water from getting under it or the spray skirt. For warmer conditions, wetsuit shorts and a short-sleeve cagoule may be enough without a shirt underneath.

- *Footwear* that is commonly worn includes wetsuit boots, shoes designed for watersports, or strapped sandals. Protection for the feet from sharp rocks and slippery surfaces help keep you safe in white water or on shore.

- Along with clothing, *float bags* are frequently secured in white-water kayaks to improve their buoyancy.

Safety equipment for white-water trips is also quite specialized. Having it on hand is one thing, but every kayaker needs to know how to use it, both as a rescuer and as a victim.

- *Throw ropes* especially designed for water sports are vitally important. The floatable, brightly colored rope is coiled in a nylon bag that can be thrown to a swimmer for rescue. The special design of white-water PFDs enables the swimmer to attach the rope with a karabiner to his back and the rescuer to attach it to a specially designed rescue belt that can be quickly released in the event of trouble.

- *Climbing slings* can be used on calm water as assistance in re-entering a capsized kayak. On white water as well as calm water, they are invaluable for towing another kayak and securing paddles and other equipment.

A ***folding river knife*** is needed to quickly release a rope or small obstruction, and a folding garden pruning saw can assist in a rescue from a downed branch or strainer.

How the Water Moves

The study of a river's currents and geological features is a science by itself. Many features play a role in determining just how the water flows at any given point, so it is important to have some understanding of what they look like and what it means to your progress downstream.

- **Current**: The water in a river basically flows downstream. It is not at a steady rate, however. The water in the center of the channel moves faster than the water along the banks, and the water slightly below the surface level moves faster than the other layers. This has obvious implications for speed of travel, especially when considered in terms of bends and obstacles in the river.

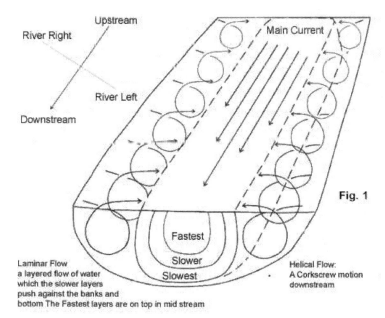

- **Bends**: When the river rounds a bend, the main current heads to the outside of the curve leaving very little margin of slow water. On the other hand, the margin of slow water around the inside of the bend is much wider. This is where the paddler should be aiming – just downstream of the inside curve – to avoid being forced into the opposite bank or becoming entangled in debris that has been deposited there.

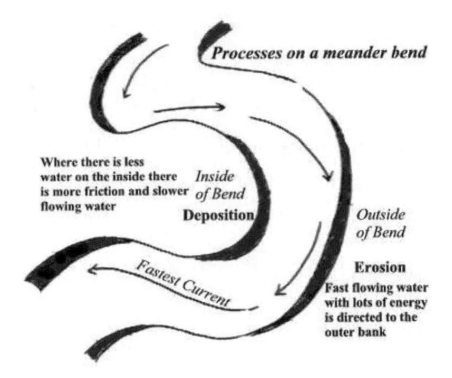

Processes on a meander bend

Where there is less water on the inside there is more friction and slower flowing water

Inside of Bend

Deposition

Outside of Bend

Erosion

Fast flowing water with lots of energy is directed to the outer bank

Fastest Current

- **Chutes and V-shapes**: A chute occurs when the water is constricted between two points. Narrow chutes usually appear between large rocks or an outcropping and rocks. The water level usually drops through this area and waves form around the obstructions. The paddler should always aim away from the upstream wave and follow the downstream V. A feature that constricts a significant section of the river's width will cause standing waves as the moving water is affected by the forced currents of water trying to get around the constriction. The paddler needs to be prepared for this, and surfing the kayak ahead of a swell is not only effective, but fun!

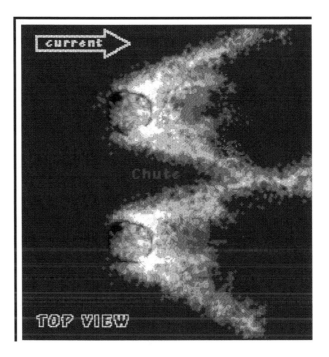

- **Holes (hydraulics)**: When water rushes over a large obstruction, it flows quickly to the base of the rock and most goes on down the river. Because of the size of the obstacle, water does not circulate in from the sides to fill the void, so some of the water from the down-flow 'boils up' into a neutral zone of water that is neither moving up- or downstream. Some of that water circulates back to the rock where it combines with the new water flowing over the top. This pattern of re-circulation creates a hole that can trap a kayak sideways alongside the rock or form a type of wave that the kayak can run as it continues down the river. Some kayakers ferry out of the hole only to get back in it for the ride. As you approach this type of obstruction, look just downstream and determine what the water of the boil looks like. If it resembles a wave with water splashing up, the hole will be easier to handle. Flat-looking water indicates a stronger hydraulic.

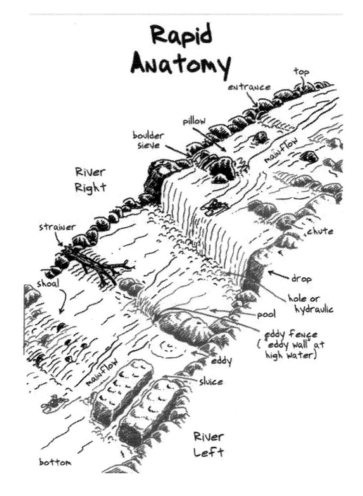

- **Eddies**: These are deceptively calm water spots on the downstream side of an obstacle around which the water is flowing. As the water rushes past, a void is left and some of the flowing water recirculates upstream to fill it in. An upstream current is created, and the line between the up- and downstream water is called *the eddy line*. The greater the difference in the rate of the two flow directions, the eddy line may actually become a wall with a different elevation in the two currents. This is much more difficult and can easily tip an unsuspecting paddler. Eddies are generally friendly and can be used as brief rest spots as you are navigating a long stretch of rapids. The lower edge of the eddy is also a good place to enter the water or move onto the shore in an otherwise fast-moving section of the river.

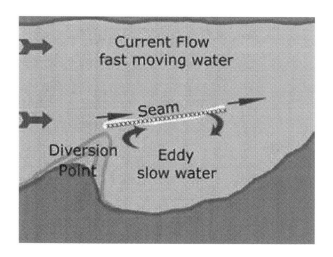

Using the River

As you develop an understanding of the nature of the river currents and the water's reactions to obstacles, you will begin to see how they can help the downstream course of the kayak instead of presenting a danger. In other words, you can see how to **go with the flow and use the force of the river to propel you.**

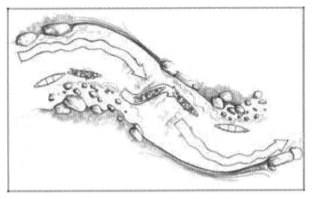

Three maneuvers are commonly used on white water.

- The **break out** is used to get out of the current into an eddy. The kayak heads downstream to the eddy line at a moderate angle, about 45 degrees. At that point, three techniques can be used to turn the kayak upstream in the eddy.

  1. Using a bow rudder planted in the eddy, lean upstream as the kayak begins to spin on the eddy line. Hold the bow rudder through the turn and change it to a power stroke to move up into the eddy. Once mastered, this is the method used by experienced paddlers.

  2. A low brace (detailed in Chapter 7) can be planted on the upstream side of the kayak as you reach the eddy line to provide stability as the kayak spins on the line, and you lean upstream to capitalize on edging. Beginners find this method to work the best.

  3. It is possible to break out with no special strokes by using good leaning techniques. As you approach the eddy line at a moderate angle, begin an upstream lean as you reach the line and continue the lean until you are facing upstream in the eddy. This is also a more advanced move, but good practice for learning the feel of the kayak in different water conditions.

- The **break in** is the opposite of the break out, and the forces of the water are reversed. You begin by paddling upstream to the eddy line, again at a 45-degree angle to the eddy line, with enough speed to get you across the line. You do not want to have the conflicting flow of the eddy line catch and spin the kayak because you will probably find yourself in the water.

  1. Advanced paddlers will lift the upstream side of the kayak and reach forward to plant a bow rudder in the downstream current. This plant should be held until the kayak is fully in the downstream current and the plant can be turned into a paddling stroke with a turn of the wrists.

  2. The best method for learners is the low brace. You need to paddle up to the eddy line and apply an eddy-side sweep stroke to turn the kayak. Immediately, apply a low brace in the downstream flow and use it for support as you lean away from the current so it can turn the kayak into the current.

  3. Another move advanced paddlers use is the break in without using either the bow rudder or bracing stroke. In this case, you paddle across the eddy line, but accomplish the turn with appropriate leaning techniques, while continuing to paddle.

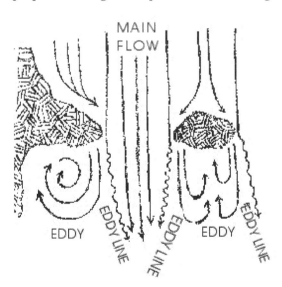

- The **ferry glide** is a skill that enables a paddler to cross the current without aiming downstream. You begin by pointing the kayak almost directly upstream and performing an upstream lift with just your knee. The rest of the crossing is done with strong forward paddle strokes. If you are planning on entering another eddy, you must switch your edge to the downstream current to cross that eddy line. Note that the upstream angle at which you enter the current is the most important factor in a successful crossing and not the use of sweep strokes. A **reverse ferry glide** is used in situations that require you to cross the current, while essentially paddling in place. With the kayak pointed downstream, the paddler uses strong backward strokes. With this technique, you can look over the water and obstacles downstream and plan your next forward line.

- The **cross** is used to move from one eddy to another that may be slightly downstream. The paddler performs a basic break in technique, but instead of turning downstream, begins to paddle rapidly across the current with a downstream lean. Upon reaching the other eddy, a quick change of edges is required as the break out technique is applied. The kayak should end up facing upstream in the second eddy.

River Hazards

Any river can present dangers to paddlers even if there is no real white water. This is where it is always good to have scouted out the river beforehand and gotten advice from local experienced paddlers.

Entrapment is the worst thing that can happen to a paddler and can occur in various ways. If you have capsized and are being swept downstream, it is critical to adopt the defensive swimming posture. That simply means to lay on your back with your feet downstream, toes pointed up if possible. If your foot or any part of your body becomes wedged in between rocks, the force of the current may keep your body pressed under the water.

Another factor in capsizing and being swept downstream is the location of the kayak. Always make sure that you are upstream from the boat so that you cannot become wedged or crushed between the boat and an obstacle. If you have to choose to hold on to the boat or the paddle, keep the paddle – the boat is much easier to find and retrieve downstream.

Misreading a **vertical drop** may cause the bow of the boat to become buried in the bottom of the river. This is especially dangerous if the force of the water flowing over the paddler's back prevents him from getting out of the kayak. Wiggling the body and trying to push with the paddle may work, but this usually requires help from others.

Strainers are hazards that water can flow through, but the openings are so small, a boat or boater cannot. Things like fallen trees or places where debris is caught between rocks need to be avoided completely. Even if the paddler runs into a strainer above the water line, the force of the water finding its way through the obstacle can drag the kayak and the paddler under the surface jamming them into the strainer. This phenomenon is usually found on the outside of a bend – that is why the correct course is just past the inside curve.

There are additional situations that can be dangerous to paddlers, a few of which will be mentioned in the next chapter. The most important advice to take from this section is to **paddle within your abilities**! A beginner in the correct environment should not be exposed to these situations. This also points to the necessity of paddling with others, especially experienced paddlers or instructors, until your paddling skills and ability to read river conditions improve. White-water kayaking is fun and exciting, but only if you can control your kayak and know how to handle the river.

Common River Sense

The first thing to realize is that **you cannot successfully kayak if you are afraid**. Fear leads to panic and that is dangerous in an emergency. Learning how to paddle correctly is the best way to alleviate fear, and practicing within your abilities provides a familiarity with the kayak and water that generates confidence for learning and experiencing more.

Planning and *information about the area* in which you choose to paddle are also invaluable for safety and to have the most fun. This should be explored beforehand using maps, charts, and recently published guidebooks that show and describe the area in detail, including river gradients, dams, or other significant obstructions and access points for emergency purposes. Talking with local river sport outfitters, conservation officers or park rangers, and other knowledgeable people can fill in details not available in print or online. Information about river level and flow are also important.

As the trip progresses, it is also a good idea to *scout ahead*. This can be done from an eddy when there is adequate visibility or by several group members beaching the kayaks and walking downstream. If you see conditions that you would not want to swim based on the assumption that you may capsize, plan to portage downstream to a suitable put in spot. **Never** enter a stretch of water you don't feel comfortable about.

CHAPTER 10 – ADVANCED KAYAKING

Preparation

The preparation for any experience involving advanced level kayaking skills is very critical. Everyone involved (obviously this should never be attempted on one's own) has to have demonstrated excellent control of the kayak in difficult situations, become proficient at all rescue skills, and researched the area to be travelled carefully and completely. The first kayakers to explore more difficult options were the slalom racers and then the freestyle competitors who had mastered specific techniques that gave them the ability try much more difficult conditions.

Each person involved in an advanced trip should carry all his own safety gear and be ready to use it without hesitation. Constant improvement of kayaks and paddles has created a situation in which more difficult maneuvers are possible to achieve, but a true understanding of the risks and one's own ability have to be acknowledged in order to avoid serious injury or death.

Sea Trips

As far as advanced kayaking on the open water is concerned, the most extreme factor is the paddler's endurance and ability to navigate tides and currents over a great distance. Just like with white-water kayaking, the paddler must understand the environment, be prepared for changing conditions, and acknowledge his abilities and limitations.

If an open-water kayaker does not already have a strobe emergency light and flares, that is the first thing he should acquire for a long trip, especially if there will be long stretches of open water far from land. GPS equipment and a marine band radio should be on board along with an air horn that can create enough sound for motorized craft to hear. A whistle is still good within the group, but in the event of an emergency or imminent collision, only a loud, piercing sound will attract adequate attention.

It is always a good idea to carry a waterproof flashlight in the event that you are delayed reaching your evening stop, but additional lighting is required for nighttime paddling and should only be attempted by competent paddlers familiar with the area and the movement of boats. For serious open-water kayakers, PFDs are made with reflective tape, and a strobe light can be clipped to the shoulder so it is visible even if the paddler is in the water. Radio and satellite beacons like those used on boats are also available, but are often set off by accident.

Kayak surfing has become popular and provides opportunities for performing some trick maneuvers as well as traditional surfboard-style wave riding. This paddler needs excellent leaning and bracing techniques as well as the ability to roll, which come from a lot of white-water experience. Some features on the river mimic the conditions encountered in surf kayaking, so it is a logical place to get the feel of the water.

Extreme White Water

This is the area of the sport where the limits are constantly being pushed. Grade 6 rapids have been successfully navigated as has running a waterfall of up to 100 feet (30 meters). This is the extreme of extreme kayaking! In these conditions, no one can help a kayaker on the water. Help is only available from the banks and down river. These members of the team should all have extensive first aid and rescue training, or arrangements could be made to also have a physician on hand.

The equipment needed for such extreme conditions is also more involved. The kayaks used are made out of plastic, are shorter, and have a dulled bow and stern. The kayaker exchanges a regular helmet for one with complete head and face coverage similar to a motorcycle helmet. Additional padding of the torso and even a back support may be worn to help prevent spinal compression. Reinforced gloves and elbow pads are also used for added protection.

Somewhat less dangerous but just as much fun, play paddling and squirt boating utilize smaller, specially shaped kayaks to perform stunts and jumps in white water. This would be the water equivalent of snowboarding and skateboarding tricks over obstacles and in the half pipe. Specially designed courses are created for these maneuvers as well as slalom racing.

Advanced Recovery and Rescue

In extreme emergencies, a complete familiarity with first aid and resuscitation techniques and the ability to contact emergency personnel are required. If this is not the group leader, it must be made clear to all members of the group who that person is. On open water, the stabilization of a kayak is essential for an injured or not breathing person to be helped.

As far as performing rescues in white-water situations is concerned, experience is the best resource along with common sense and safety consciousness for those involved in the rescue. Everyone should continue wearing a PFD and watersport shoes or sandals.

The tow rope is the only option to rescue someone from shore. In the event of having to rescue a kayak, a type of pulley system using extra line and karabiners may be necessary for added leverage and support. Because the force of the water pressing on a person or kayak is extreme, you should never try to pull with your hands. Gloves will help, but the best technique involves wrapping the rope under one arm, behind your back, and over the opposite shoulder. In this manner, you have access to the strength of your back and shoulders in addition to that of your arms. You should always consider tying the loose end of the rope around a tree and running the line through a karabiner attached to that or another tree before attempting to pull. This is called a 'vector pull.'

In the most extreme situations, an airlift may be required to rescue someone from the sea or remove them from the riverbank. The rescue helicopter would undoubtedly have personnel aboard to assist the injured paddler, so it is everyone else's role to stay calm, step back, and listen to directions from this person as they would from their own group leader.

Competitive Kayaking

Added as an Olympic sport in 1936, kayaking has grown in overall popularity ever since. There are many clubs and organizations that sponsor competitive events every year, which are well attended by avid kayakers and
spectators.

There are several different sprint and flat-water racing events where speed
is the key feature. This involves individual and multi-paddled events. The
more involved events are wild river racing, white-water slalom, and freestyle.

Slalom was developed by downhill skiers as a training opportunity in the
summer. A course is set up with gates through which the paddlers must
pass. The interesting part of this event is the different color gates. The paddler passes through the green and white gates moving downstream, but he
has to maneuver and pass through the red and white gates moving upstream! This is a test of skill, technique, concentration, and time. As an
Olympic event, slalom racing has occurred in most Olympiads since 1972.
The only reliable way to become involved with slalom kayaking is through a
club.

Free style or ***competition play kayaking*** is where paddlers can really
push the capabilities of themselves and their equipment. There are set
moves just like those in snowboarding and skateboarding that are performed for points. The kayaker takes advantage of vertical drops, holes,
boils, eddy walls, and chutes to provide the force for spinning, jumping, and
standing their craft on its end.

Extreme racing as a separate discipline grew out of the mix of white-water racing and freestyle kayaking. While not a timed race, the venue allows free-style kayakers the opportunity to show their mastery of skills in extreme white water sometimes using grade 4 and 5 rapids and up to 33 feet (10 meter) waterfalls.

CONCLUSION

Right now, you are probably anxious to get out to the water and try kayaking. It is a great opportunity for fun and exercise and is a sport that you can participate in throughout your life. You should be looking forward to getting together with some friends or joining a group or class and starting to master the skills to be safe and successful on the water! Perhaps your desire for excitement has found an outlet in the mastery of the water by engaging in extreme paddling or racing. Or maybe your need to relax and have time to reflect will be met with calm-water kayaking along the shore or a slow-moving river.

Now you are ready to utilize the information in this book as a guide to select the kayak and equipment that will be the best for the type of paddling you want to enjoy. Follow the exercise advice to be perfectly fit and ready for the physical demands of kayaking. Think carefully about safety and the rescue techniques explained in the text to stay alert and be ready for obstacles and the capsizing that will undoubtedly occur. Take advantage of the descriptions of reading a river or understanding the surf to get started and develop your own sense of the water and wind and the way they move.

The descriptions of the strokes should enable you to practice the moves in a chair and transfer them to the kayak when you get to the water. Imagine the feel of gliding across the water or rushing down a fast-moving stream and navigating around the obstacles you have read about. Experience success as you match your newfound knowledge to the actual process of paddling!

This book has provided some basic information about kayaking and resources to learn more. Let this be your first step towards enjoying the sport and recreation of paddling, but don't limit yourself! Take advantage of the knowledge and advice of professional instructors or other experienced boaters to have the best experiences possible. You now have the tools to embark on a recreational activity that you can enjoy for the rest of your life, so get out there and discover just how rewarding kayaking can be!

APPENDICES

Glossary of Terms

Aft – toward the back of the kayak

Beam – the width of the boat

Big water – rapids with a high volume of water

Blade – the end of the paddle that goes in the water

Boils – water rising up from below downstream of an obstacle

Bow – the front part of the kayak

Bow draw – a stroke used to pull the bow of the boat sideways across the water

Bow rudder – an advanced move to make a quick turn in a moving kayak

Brace – support strokes – low is safer and more common; high is more advanced and risky

Break in – move into the main current from still water, such as an eddy

Break out – move out of the main current into still water, such as an eddy

Capsize – the action of turning the boat upside down in the water

Center line – an imaginary line running from bow to stern

Deck – top of an enclosed kayak

Downstream – the usual direction of the current moving uphill to downhill, or to the sea

Draft – the measure of the amount of water displaced by the boat

Draw stroke – a stroke used to pull the kayak sideways in the water

Drop – an obvious change in water level at a particular point

Eddy – an area of basically still water that moves upstream towards a large obstruction

End grabs – the rope holds at each end of the kayak used for carrying or towing

Falls – a more significant drop in the water level, usually vertical or nearly vertical

Feather – the angling of a paddle blade

Feedback – the feeling of how the water, kayak, paddle, and paddler interact with and influence one another

Ferry glide – method of crossing the current without moving up- or downstream

Flat water – water without waves or current significant enough to affect the kayak

Flotation – extra devices used under the bow and stern decks to help the kayak float when capsized

Forward – towards the front or bow of the boat

Grade – the measure that determines the severity of rapids

Green water – unaerated water flowing around or between obstacles, not always flat

Grip – the part of the paddle that is held and the manner in which the paddle is held

Hole (hydraulic) – a water feature that can stop and hold a kayak or swimmer, usually a recirculating wave

Hull – the lower portion of a boat

Karabiner – a metal clip used by climbers that is effective for rescues and quick hookups

Keel – the bottom center of the boat running bow to stern, usually with some type of V form

Leeward – the direction toward which the wind blows

Open water – an extensive area of a lake, sea, or large river that is basically flat water

PFD – personal floatation device, life jacket, or vest to provide buoyancy to a person in the water

Pin spot – a location of a natural hazard that could lead to entrapment

Port – the left side of the boat from the perspective of the operator

Portage – carrying a boat and gear on land around an impassable section of a river or from one body of water to the next

Pour-over – where water pours over a distinct vertical drop or over and around an obstruction and forms a strong hydraulic

Power pocket – the steepest portion of a green wave, usually at its edge

Rapid – area of rough water passing over and around rocks and boulders

Recirculate – water that is repeatedly forced upstream and forced under again by the downward flow of water over an obstacle that can lead to a hydraulic feature

Rocker – the degree to which the boat's hull curves up at the ends

Roll – a method of righting a capsized boat without getting out of it

Seal launch – entering the water from an elevated position, while seated in the boat, and holding the paddle

Seams – two converging currents that frequently fold downwards at the edges

Shaft – the area of the paddle between the blades

Shoulder – the edge where a wave breaks

Siphon – a hazard where the water passes under an obstruction with no clearance

Spray deck – also known as a spray skirt – a covering, usually made of nylon or neoprene, attached to the kayak's cockpit and worn around the waist to prevent water from entering the kayak

Starboard – the right side of the boat from the perspective of the operator

Stern – the rear section of the boat

Stern rudder – a stroke used to steer, while moving forward

Stopper – a hole or recirculating wave strong enough to stop and hold a boat or swimmer

Strainer – a hazard in the water through which water flows like a sieve

Sweep strokes – paddling in a wide arc along the kayak to turn, while maintaining forward or backward motion

Throwline – a rescue rope in a bag

Upstream – the direction towards the source of the river

Volume – the amount of water flowing through rapids; the quantity of air trapped in a boat

Wet exit – the method of getting out of a capsized boat, while under water

Whirlpool – a significant water feature in which swirling water carries anything from the surface of the water to the river bed

White water – turbulent, aerated water that looks white and sprays upwards

Windward – facing into the wind, or the direction the wind is blowing from

International River Difficulty Classification

Class I Rapids: Easy

Small waves and few obstructions. Slight risk to swimmers with easy self-rescue.

Class II Rapids: Novice

Clear, wide channels where some maneuvering may be needed, but trained paddlers can easily avoid obstacles and medium-size waves. Slight risk of injury to swimmers and assistance is usually not needed.

Class III Rapids: Intermediate

Numerous irregular waves. Good paddling skills in narrow passages or around ledges and in fast current are required. Strainers, strong eddies, and powerful currents may be avoided or easily navigated. Swimming injuries are unlikely, but assistance may be needed if the paddler loses the kayak.

Class IV: Advanced

Rapids are powerful but predictable and require excellent control in the turbulent water and narrow chutes. Waves and holes may be unavoidable. Take advantage of eddies to rest or scout ahead. Advanced moves are probably required. Swimming is difficult, and the risk of danger is moderate to high. Self-rescue may not be possible, so the performance of an Eskimo roll is required. On-water rescue should only be attempted by skilled group members. This class of rapids should be scouted from land beforehand.

Class V: Expert

This is the highest classification of rapids that can be run by most competent paddlers. These rapids are violent, extremely long with significant drops, holes, narrow chutes, and many obstacles. Excellent skills – including the Eskimo roll, proper equipment, and a great deal of experience are required. Swimming is dangerous, and rescue is almost impossible. Scouting may not be possible, so the paddler must be able to adjust to any conditions instantly.

As new rapids are attempted, they may be classified as 5.1, 5.2, etc. Each point is equivalent to the difference in difficulty between 'Class II' and 'Class III' or 'Class III' and 'Class IV' – in other words, very significant.

Class VI: Extreme and Exploratory Rapids

These rapids were formerly classified as unrunnable and are only attempted by the most advanced paddlers due to the extreme nature of the waves, obstacles, and currents. Personal scouting is required, and knowledge of the stages and depths of the river is helpful. All precautions must be taken since rescue is impossible. These rapids are frequently considered suicidal.

If 'Class VI' rapids are successfully run on many different occasions, the classification may be dropped to 'Class V.'

Definitions and Classifications of Coastal Waters

Open waters:

- **Coastal offshore** – Includes any waters farther than 2 nautical miles away from the coast. Always properly prepare for heading offshore; this is a very serious undertaking, and emergency equipment provides an extra level of safety for any vessel going offshore. Having additional safety equipment allows operators to raise an alarm if there is an emergency.

- **Coastal inshore** – Includes any waters right along the coast, within a distance of 2 nautical miles.

Inland waters:

- **Enclosed waters** – Includes waterways opening up towards the sea, such as estuaries, inlets, or bays.

- **Inland waters** – Includes waterways closed off from the sea, such as lakes and rivers.

Water Class Definitions as listed by the Sea Kayak Guides Alliance of BC (British Columbia):

Class I: Includes waters that provide easy landings and access to land-based assistance due to limited wind effect and minor to no current.

Class II: Includes waters that provide light surf beaches and easy-moderate landings from short crossings, where a paddler will see moderate wind effects and gentle-moderate, mostly non-turbulent, currents.

Class III: Includes exposed waters that provide difficult landings due to moderate-strong, mostly turbulent, currents and moderate-strong wind effects, where a paddler will see ocean swells, surf beaches, and longer crossings.

Class IV: Includes waters that provide very difficult landings due to strong-turbulent currents and wind effects, where a paddler will see rugged, exposed coast and uninhabited surf beaches with large swells and much longer crossings.

Environment and Etiquette

Since most recreational paddling (as opposed to competitive paddling) occurs in natural conditions, it is the responsibility of every paddler to follow the 'Leave No Trace' doctrine to preserve the beauty, safety, and health of the environment. The bulk of the mission statement of the *Sierra Club* (at www.sierraclub.org/policy) sums it up very well:

"To explore, enjoy, and protect the wild places of the earth; To practice and promote the responsible use of the earth's ecosystems and resources; To educate and enlist humanity to protect and restore the quality of the natural and human environment; and to use all lawful means to carry out these objectives."

Following the philosophy of leaving no trace means more, however, than not littering. It is a conscientious effort to leave the land and water as undisturbed as possible. The *Leave No Trace Center for Outdoor Ethics* (at lnt.org) has seven basic principles to achieve that goal:

Plan Ahead and Prepare

Adequate trip planning and preparation helps backcountry travelers accomplish trip goals safely and enjoyably, while simultaneously minimizing damage to the land. Poor planning often results in miserable campers and damage to natural and cultural resources. Rangers often tell stories of campers they have encountered who, because of poor planning and unexpected conditions, degrade backcountry resources and put themselves at risk.

Why Is Trip Planning Important?

- It helps ensure the safety of groups and individuals.
- It prepares you to Leave No Trace and minimizes resource damage.
- It contributes to accomplishing trip goals safely and enjoyably.
- It increases self-confidence and opportunities for learning more about nature.

Seven Elements to Consider When Planning a Trip

- Identify and record the goals (expectations) of your trip.
- Identify the skill and ability of trip participants.
- Gain knowledge of the area you plan to visit from land managers, maps, and literature.
- Choose equipment and clothing for comfort, safety, and Leave No Trace qualities.

- Plan trip activities to match your goals, skills, and abilities.
- Evaluate your trip upon return note changes you will make next time.

Other Elements to Consider

- Weather
- Terrain
- Regulations/restrictions
- Private land boundaries
- Average hiking speed of group and anticipated food consumption (leftovers create waste which leaves a trace!)
- Group size (does it meet regulations, trip purpose and Leave No Trace criteria?)

Planning for one-pot meals and light weight snacks requires a minimum of packing and preparation time, lightens loads and decreases garbage. One-pot meals require minimal cooking utensils and eliminate the need for a campfire. Two backpack stoves can be used to cook all meals for large groups if you have two large pots (one large pot can be balanced on two stoves when quick heating is desired). Remember, a stove Leaves No Trace.

Most food should be removed from its commercial packing and placed in sealable bags before packing your backpacks. Sealable bags secure food and reduce bulk and garbage. Empty bags can be placed inside each other and packed out for reuse at home. This method can reduce the amount of garbage your group must pack out at the end of the trip and eliminate the undesirable need of stashing or burying unwanted trash.

Examples of Poor Trip Planning

A group that is inexperienced or unfamiliar with the geography of an area may put people at risk by traveling through areas susceptible to flash floods or along ridge tops vulnerable to lightning activity. Groups traveling arid lands often fail to carry adequate water or a way of purifying water from natural sources. Checking with local land managers and studying maps and weather conditions can contribute to a low-risk existence.

A poorly prepared group may plan to cook meals over a campfire only to discover upon arrival at their destination that a fire ban is in effect or that firewood is in scarce supply. Such groups often build a fire anyway breaking the law or impacting the land simply because they have not planned for alternatives. Fire bans and scarce wood supplies are signs that an area is experiencing the cumulative effects of heavy recreation use.

A group that has failed to develop good travel plans may be unable to travel as fast as expected. The terrain may be too steep or the trails too rugged. These groups often resort to setting up camp late at night, sometimes in an unsafe location. Poor campsite selection usually leads to unnecessary resource damage. In addition, the group may never even reach their planned destination.

Travel and Camp on Durable Surfaces

The goal of travel in the outdoors is to move through natural areas while avoiding damage to the land or waterways. Understanding how travel causes impacts is necessary to accomplish this goal. Travel damage occurs when surface vegetation or communities of organisms are trampled beyond recovery. The resulting barren area leads to soil erosion and the development of undesirable trails. Backcountry travel may involve travel over both trails and off-trail areas.

- Durability refers to the ability of surfaces or vegetation to withstand wear or remain in a stable condition.
- Frequency of use and large group size increase the likelihood that a large area will be trampled, or that a small area will be trampled multiple times.

Dispose of Waste Properly

Human Waste

Proper disposal of human waste is important to avoid pollution of water sources, avoid the negative implications of someone else finding it, minimize the possibility of spreading disease and maximize the rate of decomposition.

Cat Holes

Cat holes are the most widely accepted method of waste disposal. Locate cat holes at least 200 feet (about 70 adult steps) from water, trails and camp. Select an inconspicuous site where other people will be unlikely to walk or camp. With a small garden trowel, dig a hole 6-8 inches deep and 4-6 inches in diameter. The cat hole should be covered and disguised with natural materials when finished. If camping in the area for more than one night, or if camping with a large group, cat hole sites should be widely dispersed.

Select a cat hole site far from water sources, 200 feet (approximately 70 adult paces) is the recommended range.

Follow these steps to dig a cat hole.

- A small garden trowel is the perfect tool for digging a cat hole.

- Dig the hole 6-8 inches deep (about the length of the trowel blade) and 4-6 inches in diameter. In a hot desert, human waste does not biodegrade easily because there is little organic soil to help break it down. In the desert, the cat hole should be only 4-6 inches deep. This will allow the heat and sun to hasten the decay process.

- When finished, the cat hole should be filled with the original dirt and disguised with native materials.

Avoid areas where water visibly flows, such as sandy washes, even if they are dry at the moment. Select a site that will maximize exposure to the sun in order to aid decomposition. Because the sun's heat will penetrate desert soils several inches, it can eventually kill pathogens if the feces are buried properly. South-facing slopes and ridge tops will have more exposure to sun and heat than other areas.

Latrines

Though cat holes are recommended for most situations, there are times when latrines may be more applicable, such as when camping with young children or if staying in one camp for longer than a few nights. Use similar criteria for selecting a latrine location as those used to locate a cat hole. Since this higher concentration of feces will decompose very slowly, location is especially important. A good way to speed decomposition and diminish odors is to toss in a handful of soil after each use. Ask your land manager about latrine-building techniques.

Toilet Paper

Use toilet paper sparingly and use only plain, white, non-perfumed brands. Toilet paper must be disposed of properly! It should either be thoroughly buried in a cat hole or placed in plastic bags and packed out. Natural toilet paper has been used by many campers for years. When done correctly, this method is as sanitary as regular toilet paper, but without the impact problems. Popular types of natural toilet paper include stones, vegetation and snow. Obviously, some experimentation is necessary to make this practice work for you, but it is worth a try! Burning toilet paper in a cat hole is not recommended.

Toilet Paper in Arid Lands: Placing toilet paper in plastic bags and packing it out as trash is the best way to Leave No Trace in a desert environment. Toilet paper should not be burned. This practice can result in wildfires.

Tampons

Proper disposal of tampons requires placing them in plastic bags and packing them out. Do not bury them because they don't decompose readily and animals may dig them up. It will take a very hot, intense fire to burn them completely—campfires are not an adequate solution.

Urine

Urine has little direct effect on vegetation or soil. In some instances, urine may draw wildlife which are attracted to the salts. They can defoliate plants and dig up soil. Urinating on rocks, pine needles, and gravel is less likely to attract wildlife. Diluting urine with water from a water bottle can help minimize negative effects.

Other Forms of Waste

"Pack it in, Pack it out" is a familiar mantra to seasoned wildland visitors. Any user of recreation lands has a responsibility to clean up before he or she leaves. Inspect your campsite and rest areas for trash or spilled foods. Pack out all trash and garbage.

Wastewater

To wash yourself or your dishes, carry water 200 feet away from streams or lakes. Scatter strained dishwater. Hand sanitizers that don't require rinsing allow you to wash your hands without worrying about wastewater disposal.

For dishwashing, use a clean pot or other container to collect water, and take it to a wash site at least 200 feet away from water sources. This lessens trampling of lakeshores, riverbanks and springs, and helps keep soap and other pollutants out of the water. Use hot water, elbow grease, and soap if absolutely necessary. Strain dirty dishwater with a fine mesh strainer before scattering it broadly. Do this well away from camp, especially if bears are a concern. Pack out the contents of the strainer in a plastic bag along with any uneaten leftovers.

In developed campgrounds, food scraps, mud and odors can accumulate where wastewater is discarded. Contact your campground host for the best disposal practices and other ways to Leave No Trace at your campsite.

Soaps and Lotions

Soap, even when it's biodegradable, can affect the water quality of lakes and streams, so minimize its use. Always wash yourself well away from shorelines (200 feet), and rinse with water carried in a pot or jug. This allows the soil to act as a filter. Where fresh water is scarce, think twice before swimming in creeks or potholes. Lotion, sunscreen, insect repellent and body oils can contaminate these vital water sources.

Leave What You Find

Minimize Site Alterations

Leave areas as you found them. Do not dig trenches for tents or construct lean tos, tables, chairs or other rudimentary improvements. If you clear an area of surface rocks, twigs or pine cones replace these items before leaving. For high impact sites, it is appropriate to clean up the site and dismantle inappropriate user-built facilities, such as multiple fire rings and constructed seats or tables. Consider the idea that good campsites are found and not made.

In many locations, properly located and legally constructed facilities, such as a single fire ring, should be left in place. Dismantling them will cause additional impact because they will be rebuilt with new rocks and thus impact a new area. Learn to evaluate all situations you find.

Avoid Damaging Live Trees and Plants

Avoid hammering nails into trees for hanging things, hacking at them with hatchets and saws, or tying tent guy lines to trunks—thus girdling the tree. Carving initials into trees is unacceptable. The cutting of boughs for use as sleeping pads creates minimal benefit and maximum impact. Sleeping pads are available at stores catering to campers.

Picking a few flowers does not seem like it would have any great impact and, if only a few flowers were picked, it wouldn't. But, if every visitor thought "I'll just take a few," a much more significant impact might result. Take a picture or sketch the flower instead of picking it. Experienced campers may enjoy an occasional edible plant, but they are careful not to deplete the surviving vegetation or disturb plants that are rare or are slow to reproduce.

Leave Natural Objects and Cultural Artifacts

Natural objects of beauty or interest such as antlers, petrified wood or colored rocks add to the mood of the backcountry and should be left so others can experience a sense of discovery. In national parks and many other protected places, it is illegal to remove natural objects.

The same ethic is applicable to cultural artifacts found on public lands. Cultural artifacts are protected by the Archaeological Resources Protection Act. It is illegal to remove or disturb archeological sites, historic sites or artifacts such as pot shards, arrowheads, structures and even antique bottles found on public lands.

Minimize Campfire Impacts

Should You Build a Fire?

- The most important consideration when deciding to use a fire is the potential damage to the backcountry.

- What is the fire danger for the time of year and the location you have selected?

- Are there administrative restrictions from the agency that manages the area?

- Is there sufficient wood so its removal will not be noticeable?

- Does the harshness of alpine and desert growing conditions for trees and shrubs mean that the regeneration of wood sources cannot keep pace with the demand for firewood?

- Do group members possess the skills to build a campfire that will Leave No Trace?

Lessening Impacts When Campfires Are Used

Camp in areas where wood is abundant if building a fire. Choose not to have a fire in areas where there is little wood at higher elevations, in heavily used areas, or in desert settings. A true Leave No Trace fire shows no evidence of having been constructed.

Existing Fire Rings

The best place to build a fire is within an existing fire ring in a well-placed campsite. Keep the fire small and burning only for the time you are using it. Allow wood to burn completely to ash. Put out fires with water, not dirt. Dirt may not completely extinguish the fire. Avoid building fires next to rock outcrops where the black scars will remain for many years.

Mound Fire

Construction of a mound fire can be accomplished by using simple tools: a garden trowel, large stuff sack and a ground cloth or plastic garbage bag.

To build this type of fire:

Collect mineral soil, sand or gravel from an already disturbed source. The root hole of a toppled tree is one such source. Lay a ground cloth on the fire site and then spread the soil into a circular, flat-topped mound at least 3 to 5 inches thick. The thickness of the mound is critical to insulate the ground below from the heat of the fire. The ground cloth or garbage bag is important only in that it makes cleaning up the fire much easier. The circumference of the mound should be larger than the size of the fire to allow for the spreading of coals. The advantage of the mound fire is that it can be built on flat exposed rock or on an organic surface such as litter, duff or grass.

Fire Pans

A fire pan is another good alternative to a traditional campfire. Metal oil drain pans and some backyard barbecue grills make effective and inexpensive fire pans. The pan should have at least three-inch-high sides. It should be elevated on rocks or lined with mineral soil so the heat does not scorch the ground.

Firewood and Cleanup

- Standing trees, dead or alive, are home to birds and insects, so leave them intact. Fallen trees also provide bird and animal shelter, increase water holding capacity of the soil, and recycle nutrients back into the environment through decomposition.

- Stripping branches from standing or fallen trees detracts from an area's natural appearance.

- Avoid cutting or breaking branches from standing or downed trees. Dead and down wood burns easily, is easy to collect and leaves less impact.

- Use small pieces of wood, no larger than the diameter of an adult wrist, that can be broken with your hands.

- Gather wood over a wide area away from camp. Use dry driftwood on rivers and seashores.

- Don't bring firewood from home. Either buy it from a local source or gather it responsibly where allowed.

- Burn all wood to white ash, grind small coals to ash between your gloved hands, thoroughly soak with water, and scatter the remains over a large area away from camp. Ashes may have to be packed out in river corridors.

- Replace soil where you found it when cleaning up a mound or pan fire.

- Scatter unused wood to keep the area as natural looking as possible.

- Pack out any campfire litter. Plastic items and foil-lined wrappers should never be burned in a camp fire.

Safety

- Provide adequate supervision for young people when using stoves or fires.
- Follow all product and safety labels for stoves.
- Use approved containers for fuel.
- Never leave a fire unattended.
- Keep wood and other fuel sources away from fire.
- Thoroughly extinguish all fires.

Respect Wildlife

Learn about wildlife through quiet observation. Do not disturb wildlife or plants just for a "better look." Observe wildlife from a distance so they are not scared or forced to flee. Large groups often cause more damage to the environment and can disturb wildlife so keep your group small. If you have a larger group, divide into smaller groups if possible to minimize your impacts.

Quick movements and loud noises are stressful to animals. Travel quietly and do not pursue, feed or force animals to flee. (One exception is in bear country where it is good to make a little noise so as not to startle the bears) In hot or cold weather, disturbance can affect an animal's ability to withstand the rigorous environment. Do not touch, get close to, feed or pick up wild animals. It is stressful to the animal, and it is possible that the animal may harbor rabies or other diseases.

Sick or wounded animals can bite, peck or scratch and send you to the hospital. Young animals removed or touched by well-meaning people may cause the animals parents to abandon them. If you find sick animals or animal in trouble you should notify a game warden.

Considerate campers observe wildlife from afar, give animals a wide berth, store food securely and keep garbage and food scraps away from animals. Remember that you are a visitor to their home.

Allow animals free access to water sources by giving them the buffer space they need to feel secure. Ideally, camps should be located 200 feet or more from existing water sources. This will minimize disturbance to wildlife and ensure that animals have access to their precious drinking water. By avoiding water holes at night, you will be less likely to frighten animals because desert dwellers are usually most active after dark. With limited water in arid lands, desert travelers must strive to reduce their impact on the animals struggling for survival.

Washing and human waste disposal must be done carefully so the environment is not polluted, and animals and aquatic life are not injured. Swimming in lakes or streams is okay in most instances—but in deserts and other very arid areas it's best to leave scarce water holes undisturbed and unpolluted so animals may drink from them.

Be Considerate of Other Visitors

One of the most important components of outdoor ethics is to maintain courtesy toward other visitors. It helps everyone enjoy their outdoor experience. Many people come to the outdoors to listen to nature. Excessive noise, uncontrolled pets and damaged surroundings take away from the natural appeal of the outdoors.

The feeling of solitude, especially in open areas, is often enhanced when group size is small, contacts are infrequent and behavior is unobtrusive. To maximize your feeling of privacy, avoid trips on holidays and busy weekends or take a trip during the off season.

Technology continues to shape the outdoor experience. Personal preferences range from high-tech outdoor travelers, who might want to listen to music and collect images on their devices, to an anti-tech perspective that favors a minimal use of gadgets. Different strokes for different folks, but be sure to thoroughly consider how your experience is affecting the way someone else enjoys the outdoors. For example, earbuds may be a less obtrusive way to enjoy music than external speakers, but if you have the volume turned so high that you can't hear someone behind you who wants to pass, your personal preference for music will negatively affect other people.

The general assumption on a narrow trail is that hikers headed downhill will step aside to allow an uphill foot traveler to easily pass. In many places, there's an expectation that hikers will yield to equestrians, and that bicyclists will yield to both hikers and equestrians on trails. Stay in control when mountain biking. Before passing others, politely announce your presence and proceed with caution.

Groups leading or riding pack stock have the right-of-way on trails. Hikers and bicyclists should move off the trail to the downhill side. Talk quietly to the riders as they pass, since horses are spooked easily.

Take rest breaks on durable surfaces well off the designated trail. Keep in mind that visitors to seldom used places require an extra commitment to travel quietly and lightly on the land. When selecting a campsite, choose a site where rocks or trees will screen it from others view. Keep noise down in camp so as not to disturb other campers or those passing by on the trail.

Bright clothing and equipment, such as tents can be seen for long distances are discouraged. Especially in open natural areas, colors such as day-glow yellow may contribute to a crowded feeling; consider earth-toned colors (i.e. browns and greens) to lessen visual impacts. Keep pets under control at all times — Bowser is not in the wildlife category. Please pick up dog feces from camps and trails. Some areas prohibit dogs or require them to be on a leash at all times.

[©2019 by the Leave No Trace Center for Outdoor Ethics: https://lnt.org/why/7-principles/.]

Other points of etiquette are designed to make everyone's experience on the water pleasant and safe:

1. Obey all navigational rules and the launch site policies.
2. Do not encroach on private property. Use public land launching areas.
3. Respect the rights of others on the water. Share the water, avoid inappropriate language and behavior, be discreet, and don't interfere with the activities of others.
4. Stay as far away as possible from people who are fishing.
5. Do not harm or frighten wildlife and do not remove plants.
6. Consider supporting area preservation and clean up efforts to maintain the area for everyone to enjoy.

It is every paddler's responsibility to be aware of the area rules and if permits are required. Due to the popularity of the sport, many rivers are attracting more paddlers than can safely be on the river at the same time. Trips must be planned ahead or booked through outfitters who take care of the necessary permission and registration. The most important considerations for open-water kayaking are to know the navigation rules and the local patterns of boating traffic.

First Aid Kits and Medical Considerations

A well-stocked and up to date first aid kit is an essential part of a group's equipment. Items to include are:

- Non-latex rubber gloves
- CPR face shield
- Tweezers
- Razor blade
- Scissors
- Band-Aids and bandages
- Gauze pads and wrap
- Adhesive tape
- Large compresses
- Moleskin
- Thermometer
- Elastic bandages or wraps
- Antibiotic cream
- Calamine lotion
- Hydrocortisone cream
- Bee sting kit
- Burn ointment
- Antibacterial soap
- Antiseptic lotion and wipes
- Lip balm
- Insect repellant
- Sunscreen lotion
- Non-aspirin tablet or ibuprofen

First aid knowledge should include the ability to recognize and handle these likely conditions:

- Minor cuts, bruises and sprains

- Hypo- and hyperthermia
- Head injuries
- Shoulder dislocation
- Shock
- Muscle cramps
- Water in the ear (otitis externa)
- Back pain

ABOUT THE AUTHOR

Scott Parsons has been a lifelong participant in all types of water sports and camping. Starting with experiences as a Scout, then as a leader, outdoor skills were developed and have provided years of enjoyment and excitement. Canoeing and kayaking in local rivers and lakes and camping along the way have been a way of life over the course of years as a guide and for personal pleasure.

The different feelings of peace, excitement, and camaraderie are fulfilling and have added tremendous depth to life and interaction with many old and new friends. The wonders of nature feed the soul, and the need for the responsibility to protect it is a personal call to action.

Made in the USA
Middletown, DE
19 June 2024

56032542R00071